SHY

The University of Alberta Press

SHY

An Anthology

NAOMI K. LEWIS & RONA ALTROWS, EDITORS

Published by

The University of Alberta Press
Ring House 2
Edmonton, Alberta, Canada T6G 2E1
www.uap.ualberta.ca

Copyright © 2013 The University of Alberta Press

LIBRARY AND ARCHIVES CANADA CATALOGUING IN PUBLICATION

Shy : an anthology / Naomi K. Lewis and Rona Altrows, editors.

(Robert Kroetsch series)
Issued in print and electronic formats.
ISBN 978-0-88864-670-5 (pbk.).—ISBN 978-0-88864-743-6 (epub).—
ISBN 978-0-88864-744-3 (Amazon kindle).—ISBN 978-0-88864-745-0 (pdf)

1. Bashfulness—Literary collections. 2. Canadian literature (English)—21st century.
3. Canadian essays (English)—21st century. 4. Canadian poetry (English)—21st century.
I. Altrows, Rona, 1948–, editor of compilation II. Lewis, Naomi K., 1976–, editor of compilation
III. Series: Robert Kroetsch series

PS8237.B38S59 2013   C810.8'0353   C2013-904967-3
                                      C2013-904968-1

First edition, first printing, 2013.
Printed and bound in Canada by Houghton Boston Printers, Saskatoon, Saskatchewan.
Copyediting and proofreading by Lesley Peterson.

A volume in the Robert Kroetsch series.

The University of Alberta Press is committed to protecting our natural environment. As part
of our efforts, this book is printed on Enviro Paper: it contains 100% post-consumer recycled
fibres and is acid- and chlorine-free.

The University of Alberta Press gratefully acknowledges the support received for its publishing
program from The Canada Council for the Arts. The University of Alberta Press also gratefully
acknowledges the financial support of the Government of Canada through the Canada Book
Fund (CBF) and the Government of Alberta through the Alberta Multimedia Development Fund
(AMDF) for its publishing activities.

To our fellow shyniks everywhere, in admiration and solidarity.

In memory of Shirley Limbert.

Contents

xi   *Foreword*
NAOMI K. LEWIS & RONA ALTROWS

xiii *Acknowledgements*

1   Sometimes a Voice (2)
DON MCKAY

2   Silentium
STEVEN HEIGHTON

3   On Shyness and Stuttering
ELIZABETH HAYNES

11 The Shy
DAVID VAN BUREN

12 I Couldn't Reveal
ELAINE WOO

13 Say Water
NAOMI K. LEWIS

27 affect Thrum
NATALIE SIMPSON

28 that animal
WEYMAN CHAN

29 Creepmouse Manifesto
SYLVIA STOPFORTH

35 Fisher Woman
VIVIAN HANSEN

36 The Culture of Shyness
ALEX BOYD

37 Under the I
DHANA MUSIL

42 High School Shyku
LORI D. ROADHOUSE

43 Young Expressions
EVE S. KRAKOW

56 My Dear X
ELIZABETH ZOTOVA

59 Change Room
BRUCE MEYER

60 Cloak of Invisibility
MADELAINE WONG

65 Shy and I
SYDNEY SHARPE

67 Shades and Shyness
ARITHA VAN HERK

75 Secret Self
ELIZABETH GREENE

76 Disturbing the Universe
ELIZABETH GREENE

78 On Mingling
JENNIFER HOULE

80 Good for Olivier
RONA ALTROWS

85 Insecurity
MICHELINE MAYLOR

86 How to be shy
KERRY RYAN

91 Shybrightly
SHAWNA LEMAY

98 Stage Fright
CASSY WELBURN

100 As I Stand Up Here Reading, Fear Holds My Hånd
CAROL L. MACKAY

101 Are You an Introvert? Take This Simple Quiz
JANIS BUTLER HOLM

103 a more blissful orbit
STUART IAN MCKAY

104 Women Friends
BRIAN CAMPBELL

106 Shy—10 Ways
RUSSELL WANGERSKY

119 Drunk Judgement
STEVEN HEIGHTON

120 When Love Was Grey & Timid
I.B. ISKOV

121 Redder Than a Canadian Sunset
SHIRLEY LIMBERT

127 Laundry Duty
MIKE DUGGAN

128 to the red-haired girl on eighth
WEYMAN CHAN

130 Common Loon
JEFF MILLER

138 Crosswalk
JENNIFER HOULE

139 Watching My Lover
LORNA CROZIER

141 Other People's Agony
BEN GELINAS

151 It's Okay that Late at Night
WADE BELL

153 Amongst the Unseen and Unheard
DEBBIE BATEMAN

163 *Contributors*

171 *Permissions*

NAOMI K. LEWIS & RONA ALTROWS # Foreword

WE EMBARKED ON THIS ANTHOLOGY PROJECT with an
assumption: that shyness was a single authentic way of being in
the world, and a damn good way at that. Then, as submissions
rolled in, writers set us straight with the complexity of their work.
Shyness, it turns out, grows slipperier the harder we try to hold it
down. Some of us know we're shy only because everyone says so;
others know we're shy though the world tells us we're not. We're
told, explicitly and implicitly, that our shyness can and should be
"overcome." So sometimes we move to the centre of the room,
and sometimes we like the attention. Sometimes we wish with
quiet rage that gentleness were enough. Sometimes we choke—
important, unspoken words jammed painfully in our throats.

Long have the shy been misinterpreted and misunderstood.
Enough. Through the essays and poetry in these pages, thirty-nine
writers recall, lament, and celebrate our own experiences with
shyness. We define "shy" in a million shifting ways, and find that,
while shyness may be painful and raw, it may also bring empathy,
sensitivity, humour, a keen appreciation of subtlety.

Shy: each contributor to this anthology has a distinctive take
on how it feels and what it means. Shy: voices still and struggling;
well-meaning teachers hammering at child-shells; high-school
hallways cacophonous with extroverted ghouls; stages bright-lit
and microphones like guns in our faces; parties buzzing with
small talk; workplaces demanding the exposed self nine to five;
love shaking the bent cage of the heart; the usually boisterous
dumbstruck. As editors of this volume, we had hoped to find a
place for quiet, careful voices to sing and holler, but you will also
find whispers; cries of triumph and despair; nervous giggles of

the overwrought; frustrated sighs; easy laughter of those newly comfortable in their own skins.

We offer these essays and poems with no more assumptions, but with these hopes: that our fellow shyniks will find a familiar strain, that the never-shy will understand their quieter neighbours a little better, and that readers will find these pieces as striking, funny, and surprising as we do.

Acknowledgements

Shawna Lemay's essay nudged the idea for this anthology into being, and Laurel Boone, Jason Markusoff, Sydney Sharpe and Sydney Schwartz provided much-needed advice. I was Writer-in-Residence at the Calgary Public Library throughout the bulk of this book's editing, and found there time, space, enrichment, and encouragement, especially from Marje Wing. Rona Altrows came on board eagerly, with her keen eye, warmth, and experience. Thank you, all.

—NAOMI

Thank you to Naomi K. Lewis, for inviting me to co-edit, and for being such a joy to collaborate with. The journey with Naomi and our *Shy* contributors has satisfied me deeply. Thank you to Bill Paterson, my companion and consultant in all things.

—RONA

We are both grateful to Cathie Crooks, Peter Midgley, Lesley Peterson, and everyone at the University of Alberta Press, and Jonathan Meakin, for their expertise and encouragement. Our contributors' brilliance and diligence, and their patience, ensured that this book became more than we'd dared to hope. We thank everyone who sent us essays and poetry about shyness—so many moving and fierce pieces we did not have room to include.

This project was supported by a grant from the Alberta Foundation for the Arts.

Shy

DON MCKAY

Sometimes a Voice (2)

Sometimes a voice—have you heard this?—
wants not to be a voice any longer and this longing
is the worst of longings. Nothing
assuages. Not the curry-comb of conversation,
not the dog-eared broken
satisfactions of the blues. It huddles in the lungs
and won't come out. Not for the Mendelssohn Choir
constructing habitable spaces in the air, not for Yeats
intoning "Song of the Old Mother" to an ancient
microphone. It curls up in its cave
and will not stir. Not for the gentle quack
of saxophone, not for the raven's far-calling
croak. Not for *oh* the lift of poetry, or *ah*
the lover's sigh, or *um* the phrase's lost
left shoe. It tucks its nose beneath its brush
and won't. If her whisper tries
to pollinate your name, if a stranger yells
hey kid, va t'en chez toi to set another music
going in your head it simply
enters deafness. Nothing
assuages. Maybe it is singing
high in the cirque, burnishing itself
against the rockwall, maybe it is
clicking in the stones turned by the waves like faceless
dice. Have you heard this?—in the hush
of invisible feathers as they urge the dark,
stroking it toward articulation? Or the moment
when you know it's over and the nothing which you
have to say is falling all around you, lavishly,
pouring its heart out.

Silentium

STEVEN HEIGHTON

Tyutchev, 1830: an approximation

Don't speak. Stay hidden and withhold
all word of your thoughts, your dreams. Sealed
in the soul's cosmos, let them sail
like stars, through private skies, then fall
from sight before the dawn, unmarred.
Savour their arc. Don't say a word.

How can your heart pin down the phrase
by which it might be grasped? We lose,
in translation, the worlds we know.
Say a thing and it turns untrue
and leaves the deep spring's face sound-scarred.
Drink from the source. Don't say a word.

Learn to live in the self's retreat—
a cosmos forms there, where the light
can't force its way and where no sound
drowns out the spell of singing mind
and leaves it dazzled, deaf, unheard.
Take in the song. Don't say a word.

ELIZABETH HAYNES

On Shyness and Stuttering

The legitimacy of my voice, wherever I am, seems a question. In New York and then New England, I have been surrounded by people who do not talk quite as I do. I tend, like a foreigner, to resist dropping consonants...; I pronounce words as they look in print....Yet we all, in a world of mingling clans, exist in some form of linguistic exile, and most people don't stutter.

—JOHN UPDIKE,
from "Getting the Words Out," *Self-Consciousness*

WHEN I WAS NINETEEN, I left my small British Columbia town to attend the University of Victoria. I moved into residence, a co-ed hall, where there were alternating floors of boys and girls. My roommate, Avril, was a solid, lumberjack-shirt-wearing girl with punk hair and a brusque manner. She was studying Russian, and her side of the slab of wood that ran across the end of the room by the window and was our desk was always piled with weighty tomes. She wasn't in the room much. She didn't talk to me much.

I remember sitting at the desk with my little radio tuned to CFOX, reading *Candide* or *La Peste* or *Le Malade Imaginaire*, my French–English dictionary beside me, the laughter of my floor-mates' "studying" in the lounge echoing down the hallway. I'd done well in my classes in my first year at Cariboo College, even won the French essay prize (Racine's collected works) for an essay I wrote, the title of which I can't recall (was it on Sartre's *No Exit*?). In Kamloops, I spent weekends writing English essays with titles like "Symbolic Naturalism in Ibsen's *The Wild Duck*," and "The Human Predicament as Dramatized in Samuel Beckett's

Endgame," burnishing sentences for my velvet-suited hippie English prof, on whom I had a crush.

Late one night as I was burnishing a French essay, Avril came into our room. She asked me a question. I can't remember what the question was. I can't remember what I answered, but I clearly recall her saying, in a scornful voice, "Why are you always stuttering?"

I've always been shy, but I didn't and don't consider myself a person who stutters. When I was younger, however, I often had the sensation of tightness in my chest, of squeezing out the last words of a sentence. These breathing problems happened when I had to read aloud or answer a question in class and, especially, when I had to give a presentation.

I'd been willing to venture the odd comment in my college classes in Kamloops, but I clammed up at UVIC. I was intimidated by the fluency of my fellow French conversation students, many of whom had been in French Immersion or had spent summers in Quebec. I had been looking forward to taking a fiction-writing class with Audrey Thomas, because as a twelve-year-old, I'd taken summer camp with her. She'd liked my stories, then. She'd said I wrote good dialogue. But I was one of the youngest in her UVIC class, so I sat silently, listening to the older, worldlier students explain their motivations and themes (in case we'd missed them). They wrote about drug addiction, death, and divorce. You were supposed to "write what you know," and I didn't know about any of those things. I can't remember what I wrote about. Childhood, maybe? I do remember going to an end-of-the-year party at Audrey's apartment. I sat at the edge of the group, acting out a classic example of Joseph Sheehan's "approach-avoidance" theory of stuttering (both wanting to talk and not wanting to talk in equal measure), wondering how long I had to stay and when I could leave without being rude.

"I still feel Elizabeth needs much encouragement to give her a true feeling of confidence in her own abilities. She has done delightful and original work. I think she may always find it hard to have confidence in her own abilities," wrote a former teacher on my report card. My prescient kindergarten teacher. She went on to say I might have trouble with transition to grade one but that "a sympathetic teacher recognizing [my] ability should be able to overcome this."

I apparently made the transition to grade one well. I liked school. I was recommended to skip grade two, but at the end of the year we moved to Vancouver. In Vancouver, it turned out I wasn't to skip a grade. In fact, I was enrolled in a special remedial arithmetic class which involved learning to count in fives and tens with blue and orange coloured rods and cones—something all Vancouver children mastered by the end of grade one, evidently. And though I was crazy about reading and books, I was acutely aware of being in only the "second highest" reading group there.

I had a babysitter I loved, though, who taught me French. She made me a book with magazine pictures, the corresponding words carefully labelled in French. I practised saying those words over and over.

At the end of grade two, we moved to Kamloops. Encouraged by my grades three and four teachers and my mom, I started writing stories. Mom subscribed to the Saskatchewan newspaper of her childhood, the *Western Producer*. It featured a children's creative writing section to which I regularly contributed stories under the pen name Kami, after our town's rainbow trout mascot.

At home, I played with my younger sisters and the neighbourhood kids, but I would also often sneak off to find a quiet place to read and write. When I was ten, we went to Gabriola Island for our summer vacation. I found a big, hollowed-out rock on the beach, which I could line with towels and pillows to make a cozy nook. Paradise, I thought; no pesky younger sisters to bother me and a stack of Nancy Drews to read. When we visited my aunt, uncle, and seven cousins in their old stone house in Prescott, Ontario, I discovered many of the rooms had window seats that could be lined with pillows and blankets. If I pulled the velvet curtains closed and was very quiet, I could read and write for hours, undisturbed.

After my year at UVIC, I transferred to Western Washington University in Bellingham to study Speech-Language Pathology. This was my dad's idea. He thought I could combine my love of words and languages with a profession that would allow me to "make a decent living." I rejected his other ideas—high school English or French teacher—out of hand. Teachers had to speak in front of people, whole classes of hormone-crazed teenagers. I could barely talk to one person at a time. And though I secretly wanted to be a journalist, I didn't think I'd be able to interview strangers, especially strangers who had just been in a car accident, or were injured or in pain. I also wanted to be a novelist, but knew, from my dad, that down that path lay penury.

Dad arranged for me to talk to a local speech pathologist. She said I could work with kids or adults, in a school or hospital. I enjoyed kids, one on one, and I didn't mind hospitals. So I enrolled in Speech-Language Pathology. And although I liked my classes at Western, I quickly discovered I was an introvert in classrooms full of extroverts. Did my classmates ever stop talking? I went from school to my small room in a boarding house, where, during the week, I stayed up until the early hours studying, so I could go to Vancouver on the weekends to see my boyfriend. The house was full of eccentrics: Dale, a violin maker, who had long red hair which he wore either down or piled high on his head like a debutante, and lived in the attic; Les, a cross-dressing music student who borrowed my clothes; "Disco Martin," who worked in a fish-canning plant, arrived home every night at two a.m. and cranked the Donna Summer; Kim, who insisted that Prince Charles would marry a Korean girl, most likely her. I felt a lot more comfortable in my little house of eccentrics than I did with my fellow Speech Pathology students.

I worked for a year, then went to Washington State University for my Master's Degree. The Speech Pathology graduate program at WSU was small, the profs friendly and helpful. They drank beer with us. They knew our names. In fact, Elizabeth was deemed too "formal," so I was known by my childhood nickname of "E.J." I was one of several Canadians in my program. The department head had a fondness for Canadian students, who, he maintained, kept the departmental GPA high. Though I still felt shy inside, I'd learned that my profs would listen when I talked, and the more I spoke in class, the more comfortable I became answering questions and offering my opinion.

When I was in my early thirties and working, someone gave me a book about the Myers-Briggs Personality Inventories. I read it. I did the test. I had a Eureka moment. Here was an explanation for my feelings of being different than other people, of needing to spend time on my own. I *was* different from most other people. I was an INFJ, the personality type of about one percent of the population. According to www.mypersonality.info, INFJS are "artistic and creative," "live in a world of hidden meanings," focus on fantasy more than reality (hmm, an evening with the new Michael Ondaatje novel or a party, what's to choose?), fear doing the wrong thing (yup), are observers (um-hm) and avoiders (you bet), sensitive, tend to be devoted to what they believe in (there is a reason my boyfriends were of the Leftist, placard-bearing type). Many of my good friends (whom I often had to organize, being the "J" in the group) turned out to be INFPS, another rare type.

Speech Pathology was not listed as a career suggestion for INFJS, though writer was. And yet, my dad was right. I've enjoyed Speech-Language Pathology, and it has provided me with an interesting way to make a living. Almost accidentally, I ended up specializing in the treatment of stuttering. In grad school, I was assigned to be the research assistant of Dr. Marcel Wingate, a stuttering theorist and researcher, whose standard definition of stuttering is still widely used. My first job was at the Calgary General Hospital, where I was hired because they needed someone to run the outpatient stuttering program, and no one on staff wanted to do it.

I found my adult stuttering clients an interesting and diverse group. I met people who, like John Updike, went to considerable efforts to hide their stuttering. I met people who didn't. I met introverts and extroverts. I met clients who said they'd be extroverts if talking wasn't so difficult, and, indeed, became more extroverted as their fluency improved.

I got involved with a rather militant American self-help organization called the National Stuttering Project. (They protested Michael Palin's portrayal of stuttering in the movie *A Fish Called Wanda*, Porky Pig, and other negative depictions of stuttering in the media.) I learned how stuttering and people's negative reactions to it could shape and silence a person. I read the actor

James Earl Jones's autobiography, *Voices and Silences*. Because of his stutter, Jones was essentially mute and didn't speak from the ages of six to fourteen. Then his English teacher, a former professor, challenged Jones to prove he hadn't plagiarized a poem he had written by reading it aloud. Jones did so and discovered he had an actor's voice: deep and rich and resonant.

I moved to a job in public health but continued to specialize in the treatment of stuttering. I helped the local support group, and we organized a national conference for people who stutter, called "Many Paths, One Journey." In 2002, I joined the staff at the Institute for Stuttering Treatment and Research, where I still work today.

What has kept me working in this area is the courage of my clients. The six-year-old boy who told me he would be more "curious" if he didn't stutter. The thirteen-year-old who, tired of enduring the gossipy bullying of other teenage girls which didn't change after she "told," asked her mom to pull her out of that school and get her some speech therapy. The fifty-year-old who, fed up with having some of his fellow ESL students giggle, roll their eyes, or look impatient when he spoke, stood up, wrote "stuttering" on the white board, and explained to the class what stuttering was and why it was so difficult for him to talk. He asked for their patience. He asked for their respect.

"I think a stutterer," says James Earl Jones, "ends up with a greater need to express himself, or perhaps, a greater awareness of the deep human need for expression. Being a...stutterer leaves you painfully aware of how you would *like* to say something. And I would know, as an afterthought, how I could have said this or that. But at the moment, you are too busy making the choice to speak or not to speak, to use this word or that word. The pain is in the reflection. The desire to speak builds and builds until it becomes part of your energy, your life force. But when I was a boy, speech became a wall I could not surmount."

I have come to realize what a complex problem stuttering is. Neurophysiology, genetics, learning, and environment all play a part. I have seen how deeply stuttering can affect people. I meet parents who feel tremendous guilt about their children's stuttering, who cry when I tell them that they didn't cause the problem. I meet very young children who, within a week of starting to stutter, cover their mouths and say, "Mommy, help me talk." I meet adults who, bullied as children, have gone underground, who won't mention or discuss their stuttering with anyone, not even their spouses.

Contrary to what we may see in movies like *A Fish Called Wanda*, there is no one "stuttering personality." Though the stereotype is that people who stutter are shy, timid, nervous, and lacking in confidence, studies have shown that, as a group, they are no more likely to be maladjusted than people who don't stutter, though they may, understandably, have more fears about speaking. That so many of my clients are willing to work hard to overcome those fears is testament to their strength and courage in the face of a society that still doesn't quite understand stuttering.

Sometimes my clients tell me that they want to speak perfectly, like "normal speakers." I understand the sentiment (if only I could write perfectly, like this or that author), but tell them that no one has perfect fluency. We all repeat, revise, say *um* and *ah*, hem and haw. I tell them perfect fluency can sound memorized, glib, and insincere, like the speech of a famous scientist I once heard whose rapid speech rate and hyperfluency made it difficult to absorb anything he was saying. I agree with John Updike that "people who talk too easily and comfortably, with too much happy rolling of the vowels and satisfied curling of the lips around the grammatical rhythms, rouse distrust in some atavistic, pre-speech part of ourselves; we turn off. Whereas those who stutter win, in the painful pauses of their demonstration that speech isn't entirely natural, a respectful attention, a tender alertness. Words are, we are reassured, precious."

Indeed they are. Nowadays, people often express surprise when I tell them I am shy (though, as a shy person, I don't do so routinely). "You don't seem shy," they say. And it's true. I rarely blush anymore when strangers talk to me. I can make good eye contact. These are things that I've learned. I've watched outgoing people and copied them. I've made myself enter situations I'd prefer to avoid (cocktail parties with rich, well-dressed people; actually, cocktail parties with anyone). I've joined Toastmasters. Still, in a group, I'm drawn to the people who hang back. The people who don't immediately overwhelm you with talk but who may, if they sense you are sincerely interested in them, offer a thoughtful comment or two.

In a society that values extroverts, I suggest we pay more attention to the introverts. (But let's not do so in a showy way that calls undue attention to them, please.) The quiet girl who watches her peers, then silently joins their play, showing them a better way to make that paper boat float. The little boy at the back of the class, drawing and writing in his notebook. Observe them. Find out what they're good at. They might be architects, artists, writers. Be assured, they are watching, thinking, observing. There are interesting things happening in their heads that we'll never know about unless we take the time to ask. Unless we take the time to listen.

DAVID VAN BUREN

The Shy

When his brothers trudged off
to choose their mates,
did he go too,
and from behind a tree trunk watch
the boldest one pick first,
unsure where to place his hands
before the invention of pockets.

Or did he stay put
to keep the fire going,
and shake his club
up at the moon, confused
how it could be alone
yet so sure of itself,
surrounded by the stars
that all seemed to know each other.

I Couldn't Reveal

ELAINE WOO

After school, in her older sister's pink bedroom
we stood next to the bed with the chenille spread.
She put the needle on the record,
the rhythms of *She loves you, yeah, yeah, yeah* beatled out,
arched my toes, drove me itchy to tap, tap, tap,
my torso twist and twirl.
But I pushed my shiny Mary Janes firmly
into the floor, pinned my arms to my plaid skirt.
I looked at her red curls, pin dot freckles,
upturned lips.
No. I couldn't show her.
My cheeks stung as if visited by a swarm of bees.

12

NAOMI K. LEWIS   Say Water

"ESSAY," said Miss B.

I leaned over my assignment, carefully circling the correct
answers with tight, tidy lines, trying to imitate the way the girls
sitting on either side of me did it.

"Essay!" my teacher said again, louder. I'd heard of an essay
but, in January of third grade, had never come close to reading
or writing one. Was it possible my new class was so far ahead?
It sure didn't seem like it; after all, we'd spent the last twenty
minutes matching up pictures of habitats with their animal
inhabitants.

"Essaie," said Miss B. *Try*, présent simple, as in *J'essaie. I try.
I do my best*. Also, impératif, as in, *Try!* French grammar books
used exclamation marks to indicate the imperative tone. *Try
harder! Try harder!* I had been liberated, or cast out, from my
French immersion class a month before, after a year. I had tried.
Not hard enough. I had failed. After the Christmas holiday, I was
now trying anew, in the English class.

"Ess," Miss B. cried. "Ay." I noticed with a start that I'd
forgotten about the tidy girlish circles again, and had reverted to
the loose, messy kind—shaky, amoebic, executed in one second
instead of ten. Cupping my hand over the ugliness, I tried to
erase it, but only smudged a graphite shadow across the bunny
and bat cave pictures, and crinkled the paper.

"Naomi!" said Miss B.

All my nerves cringed with the sound of my name, and I bolted
upright. Something was wrong. An eerie silence had come over
the room; I hadn't noticed it, but now I realized it had been there
for some time. All my classmates were perfectly motionless, like
statues, frozen at their desks with fat red pencils in their hands,

or walking—a boy stood on one foot, swaying with the effort to stay balanced—and some had their heads cocked, mouths open, as though in mid-word. The room felt unbearably hot, and my new multi-coloured wool sweater was stifling, a sweatbox. A straitjacket.

"Will someone please tell Naomi what s.a. means? Jenny Lefebvre?" Jenny was Miss B.'s favourite, always chosen for special tasks like handing out tests or walking people to the nurse's office.

"Suspended animation," said Jenny, before reassuming her statue pose, a Kleenex to her nose. I knew it was called a Kleenex because I'd broken down in tears a few days earlier, my nose full of snot, asking blank-faced Miss B. again and again, in my British-mid-American accent, still lingering after a year in Canada, if there were any hankies in the room.

I sat as still as I could, holding my pencil in a trembling, damp hand. The classroom seemed to have reached greenhouse temperature despite all the snow blowing around outside the window. The worst part was, I'd been lost in my own world, had believed myself safely invisible while I stood out like a fluorescent light. Once again, everyone was in on something I didn't get. I still didn't get it. s.a.—suspended animation. Stay perfectly still, in the exact position you happened to be in when Miss B. spoke the magic term. But why? Didn't animation have something to do with cartoons? And suspended was what happened to bad kids, really bad ones, kids who committed unforgivable acts of rule breaking.

Then suddenly everyone was moving, with purpose. Putting away the animal habitat assignment. Reaching into their books, their bags, opening their pencil cases. Miss B. had obviously given us specific instructions.

"Naomi?" said Miss B. "Is there a problem?"

My days of staring in blank, stark stupidity were supposed to have ended with my move from French immersion to the English class. Smarting all over with the brilliant heat of an invisible spotlight, I buried my face in my arms, the cool wood of the desk against my cheek, and squeezed my eyes shut.

When I was thirty and had just finished grad school, I found myself stranded in the prairies, unemployed and suddenly single. I wanted out, and to that end, I took a three-day course on teaching English as a second language abroad. In the afternoon of the third eight-hour day, we each taught a mock class for ten minutes; each mock teacher began by telling the others the age group and knowledge level we should assume. At that point in my life, I was confident enough speaking in public that I don't remember my own teaching attempt. The ten minutes I remember belonged to a girl who told us we were five-year-old French children, in France, in their first year of an English immersion program—all English for the whole school day. She wrote her name across the board: Ms Jackson, then showed us a series of coloured cards. She walked around the room, saying each of our names the way you would a child's, and it was our job to name the colours.

Some people didn't bother acting. When their turns came, they said, "Red" or "Orange" in their regular voices, smiling indulgently, a little embarrassed. Others used French-kid accents and sat wonkily, childlike, in their chairs.

One guy made himself the class clown, yelling, "Madame! Madame! Je sais, je sais! C'est rouge!"

Ms Jackson answered evenly each time, "In English, please, Tom. We need hands, Tom." Then she ignored him. She was good.

She came to my desk, and looking directly at me, she held up the sky-blue card. "Naomi. What colour is this?"

I stared back at her.

"What colour is this?"

I didn't move. She held the blue page a little higher and smiled encouragingly. I buried my face in my arms on the desk.

"Aww," said the blonde girl across the room, with real sympathy.

"Oh," said Ms Jackson.

I heard murmurs of appreciation at my acting prowess. But then I couldn't bring myself to lift my head. I was scared. It wasn't an act anymore; I had become a child, and Ms Jackson, younger than me in real life, was my well-intentioned teacher. My heart pounded, my face burned. I could hear her breathing, still standing there, waiting. Every eye in the room was on me, waiting to see me exposed. The longer I waited, the worse it would get. That old irony: in trying to disappear, I was making a spectacle of myself.

I lifted my head an inch and peered up.

"You can do it," said Ms Jackson.

I giggled with terror.

"What colour is it?"

"Blue," I whispered.

"Yes! I heard you! Good." Visibly relieved, she moved on.

"That was so realistic," said the blonde girl, not to me, but loud enough for me to hear.

My heart rate began to slow again, but the thud of blood through my ears grew louder as my body relocated itself. The old familiar nausea set in.

"Dude." The guy sitting next to me leaned close, his hand on my binder. I'd been joking around with him since the first day. "You really were that kid, weren't you?"

"What do you mean?"

"I could tell all along."

"You could tell...?"

He hesitated before saying it, before admitting gently that none of my jokes or eye contact had fooled him. He tightened his grip on my chair, as though to bolster me from the blow of his words. "That you were shy."

If shyness was the right word for it. And yes, there's no denying I was a shy child. Some of the things I dreaded: ordering in a restaurant; the sight of a ball flying toward me, whether soccer, base or basket; piano recitals; a lot of people talking loudly at once; being called upon to speak in class. In fact, I not only dreaded those things but also was paralyzed by the prospect of them, stunned into blank stillness.

I didn't start out shy, though. I wasn't shy until my family moved from Montgomery County, Maryland, a suburb of Washington, DC, to Ottawa, when I was seven and halfway through second grade. Until then, I was the kind of child who prefers reading to playing a sport and listens more than speaks, and I had two close friends I loved with a frenzied passion, not a wide group of acquaintances. I was also a worrier. I worried about the inevitability of death and whether there was more to life than the mundane. I believed everything I learned in school and found my comfort in following rules, in staying perfectly in sync with the world's structure, as presented by my teachers, to the extent that, on the day we learned the four food groups, I panicked because I'd only had two of them for breakfast that morning. Weak and dizzy with malnutrition, and struggling quietly to contain my tears, I was taken to the nurse's office, where I refused to listen to reason. My teacher had just said it was important to eat something from each group at *each meal*; that morning I'd had toast and jam, directly violating the imperative. I wasn't about to listen to any nurse trying to explain what a cumulative effect was. Finally they phoned my mother, who came to my rescue with a whole-wheat sandwich containing cheese, beef and lettuce, covering my bases.

But if shyness involves, by definition, self-doubt or insecurity, I was not shy. I thought the world of myself. I was impervious to insults, believing my parents' theory that the sole motivation for mocking was envy. And if I worried more than the average six-year-old, well that was just because they were all too stupid to notice the things worth worrying about. The rambunctious kids my mother wished I'd befriend were, as far as I could see, incapable of sitting still, ruled by impulse, lacking in empathy, and poor conversationalists. They were living in a giddy stupor.

In the fall when I was seven, I began my first diary. Each entry consisted of a crayon drawing, usually of a stick figure, accompanied by a sentence, also in crayon. *I will be in Canada. I will have a new teacher*, I wrote. *I will make new friends. I will learn French.* My parents had told me these things, and I was trying to convince myself they were true, to understand what they could possibly mean. These diary entries weren't essays, but the books I read every night had already given me the idea that, through writing, such an attempt was possible.

My parents had decided to put me in French immersion because they'd heard that was where all the smart kids were. We'd be living across the river from Quebec, in a national capital where French-English bilingualism was a must. But my classmates had begun learning French in kindergarten, as my sister would do. Like Ms Jackson's make-believe students, they'd begun with their toes in the shallow end. They'd learned to ask for the bathroom and to politely state their names; they'd asked each other, *Comment ça va?* and told each other, *Ça va bien, merci* (no other response was possible, even if things weren't going well at all). They sang the alphabet and learned colours, days, months, and seasons. By January of second grade, they were speaking French all throughout the school day, no English allowed. And into this no English zone, I was immersed. Immersed all at once, tossed into the deep end, where I sank like a stone.

I was not allowed to say a word in English, the only language I knew, and I sat through my days understanding nothing and rendered mute. If I dared speak aloud, I was reprimanded with the silencing, "En Français, s'il-te-plaît!" I understood what that meant, but how could I possibly translate my thoughts into French? I only knew about ten words. By trapping me in a hole where French was the only way out, the only way to make friends or pass the school year, I suppose my teacher intended to accelerate my learning.

This wasn't the first time I'd felt the force of language binding my peers together and making me different. We'd first moved from England to Maryland, and when I'd started school there, I'd struggled to change the accent my new classmates informed me I had. "Say *water!*" they begged me, over snacks. I shook my head, and practised at home the American *er*, trying and eventually succeeding to replace my *tuh* with a *derr*. But all French all the time was a lot harder than saying *water*, wahderr.

"How's it going?" My parents asked me. "How's school?"

"It's going well," I responded, dutifully. *Ça va bien*.

I almost failed second grade, and by that time I had stopped speaking altogether, even in English. I was sent to a therapist. But after the summer, back I went, into the third grade French class.

I don't know what kind of therapist I went to in second grade, whether she was a psychiatrist or a psychologist or a social worker, but she apparently couldn't find anything wrong with me, and sent me back to my French class with a clean bill of mental health and no particular advice for my parents. Today, there is no shortage of books for parents whose children are shy, introverted or highly sensitive (which may or may not be different ways of describing the same or similar traits), written by experts who treat those children, who offer them breathing exercises, helpful games, and, if nothing else works, medication. Admittedly, when I read descriptions of calm, reassuring parents playing relaxation games with their anxious or overstimulated children, I'm more than a little envious on my former self's behalf. But I'm glad I suffered through my wordless childhood before anyone coined the terms "social anxiety disorder" and "selective mutism," and started prescribing pills for them; I'm grateful I made it into adulthood diagnosis- and Paxil-free.

My parents had their own ideas about the situation. Mostly, I think, they hoped I'd grow out of it, though they worried about my homebodiness, my neediness, and the fervour and fewness of my friendships. My mother also told me, once, in a moment of frustration, "You just don't think people are worth talking to. That's all shyness is." She added, "You think people are thinking about you, but they're not." My mother was not alone in her assessment; indeed, Freudians characterize shyness as a manifestation of narcissism. And perhaps it is helpful to notice that each shy person in the room believes herself the only one, believes herself different and apart, a defect in the universe's otherwise continuous pattern, exempt, even, from the platitudes of human nature—all while, according to surveys oft-cited by the experts, nearly half of North Americans consider themselves shy. So it seems shy or sensitive people are not so much special or strange as afflicted with delusions of their own specialness and strangeness.

But the therapist I saw in 1983 was no shyness expert, and no Freudian; and neither was she a Jungian, in which case she may have mentioned Jung's correlation of social introversion with "sensitiveness," a trait he ascribed to an estimated twenty-five percent of humanity. Contemporary empirical studies have backed him up, showing that shy and introverted people tend to feel sensations acutely, to be bothered by loud noises, to retreat into daydreams and fantasies. It may have been helpful to know, when I couldn't find my voice at all, that, while Jung claimed all neurotics were sensitive, and that the trait rendered them "most useless," he also said elsewhere that the quiet and careful should cast off futile attempts to become "normal" (his term), that they had their own gifts, their own paths, which would be more difficult, but potentially just as rewarding, than the straighter ones they tended to revere. That may have been helpful to hear, but instead I was sent back to the classroom, where I sat in silence and waited in vain to find some chutzpah, to grow a spine, to stop being, as my British relatives would have said, "such a terrible wimp."

Then, after the winter break, after a year of dumb incomprehension, everyone finally gave up on me, and I was switched out of French immersion and into the English class.

⋮ That year, Jamie Lefebvre, who happened to be Jenny's older brother, often babysat my sister and me on evenings when our parents went out. He was tall, almost as tall as an adult, though he must have been about twelve, and had the same reddish complexion and thick blond hair as his sister, though his hair was short and stood up in a series of little spikes. He was shy, too; I saw this when my father asked him what made the hair stand up.

"What do you put in it?" said Dad.

Jamie smiled at the floor, searching for a trapdoor. "Gel," he said, almost as a question.

Shifting uncomfortably on her high heels, my mother grinned her nervous, pre-party grin.

"Oh!" said my father. "Gel! Well, it's very cool."

Jamie smiled at his shoes, humiliated.

My bedtime was at nine o'clock, an hour after my sister's, but Jamie always let me stay up until ten, to see the second half of a two-hour *Love Boat* special. These always seemed to be on when my parents went out, a coincidence both Jamie and I found weird. Since the only TV was in my parents' room, Jamie and I watched *The Love Boat* in there, me lying on the bed in my pyjamas, chin resting on my arms, him sitting in an armchair. During the commercial breaks, we discussed the show's plot— which couples were falling in or out of love this time, and why, and whether they had a chance. I never thought about Jamie when he wasn't around, but when we were alone, I forgot to be uneasy, forgot to be embarrassed about my opinions or solar system pyjamas, forgot to expect mockery. I handed my *Love Boat* analyses over to him and watched him consider them seriously before responding.

In one of these *Love Boat* specials, as I remember it, Vicki, the captain's teenaged daughter, falls for a tall, handsome young cruise passenger travelling with his strangely overprotective parents. Vicki and the young man are left behind on a tropical island for a whole day, which they spend frolicking, foraging, getting to know each other and falling in love. As the sun sets, the ship appears on the horizon, sailing back to pick them up. Vicki and the boy embrace; they kiss; they prepare to kiss again, more seriously this time.

"Wait!" The boy turns his head, distraught. "Vicki, there's something you need to know. Something about me."

"About you?"

"I'll understand if you can't accept this, can't be with me..."

"What is it?"

"Vicki, I'm—I'm retarded."

Close-up of Vicki's face, inner turmoil written all over it. Commercial break.

Jamie and I turned to each other, baffled. The guy was a great conversationalist, fun to be around, beyond socially adept. What did he mean, retarded? And why would Vicki care?

But Vicki did care. In the last segment of the show, she parted ways with the dashing young retard forever, explaining that she just couldn't handle it. He had no hard feelings; he understood; he only felt bad for not telling her sooner.

Jamie let me stay up even longer than usual, to discuss the plot's absurdity.

"I don't get it," I said.

"Me neither. I mean, if they love each other..."

"I know."

"And she couldn't even tell..."

"I know—and how is he retarded? If he seems fine?"

"Yeah..."

I ran to my room as my parents' car pulled into the driveway, to lie awake trying to figure it out alone, without the benefit of Jamie's advanced age and insight. In French, I'd learned, the verb *retarder* meant to delay, to make late or to set back.

J'ai été retardé meant, I was held up. *Ma montre retarde* meant, My watch is slow. So, did *Je retarde* mean, I am slow? That seemed right, with my mind's tendency to quiver in each calamitous moment, gears straining.

Just a few days before, I'd found myself alone in the school washroom with Sally, a popular girl in my class. This Sally had an even-featured freckled face, dark hair, trouble with math and spelling, and no inhibitions. Some days she wore eyeliner, though I'd heard her claim she put it on as a joke the night before and couldn't get it off, and at recess, she was always the first to kiss the boys chased and pinned down by her friends. Though I didn't like anything in particular about her, I longed to be her friend. Bolstered by a good grade I'd just received and the English class's promise of a new start, I chatted with Sally for five straight minutes, by the sinks.

"Why don't you ever talk?" she asked, as I turned to leave.

I shook my head, waiting for words to explain.

"I didn't know you *could* talk," she went on. "I thought you were retarded." She said this easily, seemingly without malice, which was worse than if she'd said it to be mean. She was telling the truth. By retarded, I knew she meant mentally sub-par and socially disastrous. My affliction was no "learning challenge," but something more elusive that made me fundamentally uncool and unable to understand why. I was unacceptable. Unfriendable. Hopeless.

⋮ Five years later, when I'd just finished junior high, my sister and I spent three weeks of our summer holiday at our grandparents' house, and one afternoon our older cousin, Zarah, who lived nearby, came over to swim with us. I practised my back dives for a while, then sat beside Zarah in a deck chair, helping myself from the bowl of nuts Oma had brought out and writing descriptions in my diary—descriptions of Opa working in the garden, of the trees and the fence, and of the cool blue water, of the sensation of diving in. I held myself to writing at least one or two of these descriptions every day, partly because L.M. Montgomery's character, Emily, did similar things, and ended up being a writer, and partly because it was deeply satisfying. Satisfying because I found written words so much more accurate than anything I ever said out loud. And satisfying because, after all, when one writes *water*, there is no accent, no squeaky, little-girl stammer. In the written word, in that attempt for precise expression, there is dignity.

"So, did you like grade eight?" my cousin said. "Were there any cute boys in your class?"

"Not really."

"Are you excited to start high school?" said my cousin.

"I guess."

I longed to tell Zarah the truth, that I was no more excited about high school than I would have been to travel to Pluto—just vaguely terrified and mostly numb, the way one is when faced with the unimaginable. But I didn't know how to explain that grade eight had happened just alongside me, exhausting and impenetrable. That I'd eaten alone at lunchtime, and at recess hid in the bathroom or sat on the grass, watching. She didn't even suspect I'd stayed home at least once a week to lie in bed all day, drained and nauseous, sleeping and sipping broth as though I had the flu; and *the flu* is what my mother and I persisted in calling it. Zarah was accepting me under false pretences, and I wished I could tell her, *There's something about me you should know*. But what was this something; how could I describe it? *I'm unpopular* barely scratched the surface. That I was shy, she'd probably figured out. *I'm retarded* seemed to strike deeper into the matter.

At the end of the school year that June, some of my class-mates, whom I'd been with for three years, had made a yearbook. They pasted all our school photographs on facing pages, and wrote at the top, *We Will Remember*.... Each student got a caption. *Amanda and her daring; Laura and her laughter; Alex and his cuteness.* Under my photo was written, *Naomi and her silence.* At the last minute, they generously changed it to *Naomi and her mystery.* What bothered me wasn't the caption, but the photograph. I would have rather they left it out entirely. It wasn't true that they'd remember me; how could they, when I'd made myself so absent?

We were each asked to write a sentence or two to accompany our photograph and characterization, and I examined the black-and-white image, took in my strained smile and dorky striped shirt, my jutting collarbone and tufty hair, and wrote, *Please don't remember me this way.* Even as I wrote that sentence, to be typed up and reproduced, recorded for perpetuity, I must have felt, tightening around my throat, the noose of self-fulfillingly prophetical paradox—instead of achieving invisibility, I was exposing myself again, was wearing the very quality I wished to hide like a flashing red light.

According to the contemporary studies I have read, however, ten out of the twenty-three students in that classroom likely considered themselves shy, or do now, in retrospect. So how did the other nine resist exposing themselves so? How did they avoid being remembered for their silence? Did they, indeed? Looking back, I see one loud girl proclaim herself president of the yearbook committee, and I see a small crowd in identical outfits coalesce around her. I see a lot of carefully set faces. I see Mark, the boy next to me, stare intently at his hands when the teacher looks for volunteers. What did the yearbook say we'd remember about Mark? I forget, now. I see the Hispanic girl— the only one at the school as far as I know—lean low over her notebook, cupping her hand around whatever's she's drawing. She speaks only when questioned, in mumbled, heavily accented monosyllables. Once she glances up, and our eyes meet, briefly, before we both look away. The yearbook will command that we always remember *Karla and her hair*, which is curly, short and unstylish, with a long, braided rat-tail at the back.

Still, none of this quite gets at the questions—why do half of us call ourselves shy; what do we mean? And why is it so quickly assumed, especially in the age of "social anxiety disorder" and "social phobia," that we ought to focus our efforts on becoming yearbook-committee president types? Many of the advice books cite a study that found shy Chinese children the most popular among their peers, and shy Canadian children the least popular among theirs. In fact, the Chinese word for what we call shyness translates, *has understanding*. The experts usually mention also that Japan boasts the most shy people, per capita, in the world, and Israel the fewest. The advice-givers' biases colour what they say about all this, either imagining Asia as a haven for the quiet and watchful, or describing emotionally broken Japanese children cowering in shame while the joyous Israelis hold their emotionally healthy heads high. In any case, what the experts agree on is that, when in Israel, or in the US or Canada, you'd better hope you're not shy, especially if you're a child. And if you are shy, you need, depending on whom you ask, either a big hug or a swift kick in the pants.

⋮ There's a scene at the beginning of the film *Hilary and Jackie*, in which a young Jacqueline du Pré encounters a strange woman who tells her a secret. At the end, we see that scene again. The woman is Jackie as an adult, a ghost, and she tells her younger self, "Everything's going to be all right." I can't resist the appeal of that fantasy, of reaching back to my former, smaller self, to reassure. When I imagine encountering that Naomi, I tell her that half the people in every room feel something like she does. I meet her solemn gaze and promise that she will, slowly, grow a thicker skin, one she'll have to sustain all her life with humour and good company and measured solitude. I tell her that she'll grow up to have the life she wants, albeit infused with two-faced longing—to be granted privacy, and to be understood.

But I also tell her that life itself is immersive, a series of shoves off the highest diving board. And what I believe now is that some of us are simply faster adapters than others, more adept at finding gravity and getting our heads above water; others are held up, slowed down, and we learn that calling out, *Wait!*

Time out! is of no use at all. Even now a feeling comes over me sometimes that I, like *The Love Boat*'s fundamentally unlovable cruise passenger, no matter how normal I may look and act, carry this trait as an indelible fact. *There's something about me*, I want to tell people who seem to accept me anyway. *Something about me you should know.* But then maybe, after all, it's just that I—and that so many of us—need to shy away sometimes, to shut our eyes tight against the prismatic distortion of the depths, to hold our breath, animation suspended, before surfacing and trying for words, a language, an attempt to adequately express the latest world taking its shape.

NATALIE SIMPSON

affect Thrum

We have floundered and basted. Our portions have multiplied.
We are sated but repenting. We are lost to our innermost rhythm.
Our senses are surfeit. Our form is buffeted.

A light pulse has led us sparing. We have not sought stability.
Our uncertainty has charmed us. We are as a gluttonous lover.
And yet we have been wrenched. We have contorted. We atone.

Flimsy surrendering baits us. Stubborn thickets spring to our
mercy. Sabotage entices our lean baselessness. We hover fearing.

Our signal is a study in calm. Loop upon loop has cocooned.
We have endeared ourselves to our other selves. Our clamour
subsides. We are burgeoning.

that animal

WEYMAN CHAN

crying myself silly
when the barn doors of the orphanage
    closed in on my sister and I
    I became that animal
who chews off its memory
and limps away
like all orphanages the other
animals bite   run   return
    faces
    swallowed by an unclaimed dark
    our foster mom claimed us
    she wore a tartan that breezed
my heart to hide in
that stopped so I hid
    in tree shade near the garage
    next to the hens
    what should I have missed if it wasn't here
    to hold me
can't say
can't ask
    I'd bite others
easily stab them
with pencils after learning
what it is to cry out for an other
what would
any unfinished
    monster do to find out
    how it cares
    as thoroughly as it learns how
    to

SYLVIA STOPFORTH

Creepmouse Manifesto

It need not frighten you; it is a nothing of a part, a mere nothing, not
above half a dozen speeches altogether, and it will not much signify
if nobody hears a word you say, so you may be as creepmouse as you
like, but we must have you to look at.

—JANE AUSTEN, *Mansfield Park*

SO, I DID A LITTLE RESEARCH, and found that there are a lot
of angry extroverts out there.

Why are they angry?

Well, they're tired of being snubbed by a handful of self-
absorbed wallflowers who can't be bothered to respond to a
simple, friendly "hello." They feel, moreover, that there is no such
thing as shyness, that this term is nothing more than an excuse,
a cover-up, for apathy at best or out-and-out rudeness at worst.

Indignant, I set out to write a ringing defense of The Shy, to
sing the praises of the calm, the quiet, those who spurn the
limelight. I was determined to dismantle those condescending
definitions—so often written, it seems, by perplexed extroverts—
which characterize us as fearful, anxiety-ridden, timid, uneasy,
withdrawn, and inhibited. I'd follow this up by pointing out that
many successful, famous people have been labelled "shy." Abraham
Lincoln and Eleanor Roosevelt were apparently among the naturally
retiring. As are Don Rickles and Nicole Kidman.

To refute those who claim shyness does not exist, I'd drop the
names of two universities in the United States that have "Shyness
Institutes" entirely devoted to the study of this allegedly fictitious
concept. I'd cite research conducted in the 1970s (an honest
decade, not given to dissembling) which revealed that "only

about seven percent of Americans surveyed indicate that they have never experienced shyness in their entire life....Thus, shyness is a pervasive phenomenon; if you are shy, you are not alone."

Of course, if you are shy, you may prefer to be alone, but that's neither here nor there.

I had structure. I had headers. I had data affirming that shyness exists, is widespread, has not stopped people from excelling in life, and often brings in its train all manner of valid and valuable qualities.

There was just one problem: none of it mattered. It all rang hollow.

So instead, I'll just share a story.

It was Wednesday.

Day four.

Nearing the halfway mark.

Just three days to go.

They announced we'd be doing archery after breakfast. Granted, the potential for public humiliation was there, yet the prospect didn't fill me with dread. After three days and nights of the never-ending presence of others, the non-stop chatter of mosquito-bite-ridden, cabin-fevered girls with whom I had nothing in common aside from the year of our birth, I suppose I'd become accustomed—or, rather numbed—to their constant *there*-ness.

And unlike softball, soccer, or the dreaded skits, archery was not inherently a team activity. At least there was the suggestion of solitariness about it.

But when we got down to the archery butts, the other shoe dropped. A noisome, jostling, herd of boys would be joining us, taking turns in some ill-conceived, prepubescent battle of the genders.

My fight-or-flight instinct kicked in, and with a whispered word to my camp counsellor, I fled to the only refuge I could think of. The tiled, spidery building, redolent of mould and chlorine, was the only spot where one could, on occasion, find a moment's respite from the relentless group-think of the place.

Through some great stroke of luck, the washroom was empty, the rows of stalls with their sweating pipes abandoned. I leaned on a sink and tried to calm down enough to calculate how long I'd need to wait. I indulged in a moment's fantasy, picturing an alternate-universe me sauntering casually back to the group just in time to see the boys disappearing and the bows being put away, and to express my aw-shucks disappointment at having missed out on all the fun.

Footsteps crunched on the gravel path.

I retreated to the far wall.

Someone entered the building.

I slipped into one of the stalls, barely breathing as I turned the lock.

My counsellor called my name.

I briefly considered the possibility that she would overlook me, that I could avoid notice simply by remaining silent.

"Is everything all right?" she called, standing outside my cubicle door. I could see her tanned feet in their bright pink flip-flops.

I could fake some sort of gastric distress. If I was convincing enough, she might leave without me; she might even leave quite quickly. But doubtless she'd report me to the camp nurse, or worse, to some of the other counsellors. Word would get around.

It came down to the weighing-up of potential mortifications, a calculation at which I excelled.

"Everything's okay," I answered, flushing the toilet and emerging with an attempt at nonchalance, an attempt I immediately knew to be a dismal failure.

"They're all waiting for you," she said, a small frown creasing her forehead, and my heart sank.

On the way back to the field, she tried for a friendly, conversational tone. But I could hear the underlying bafflement, the familiar impatience with my apparently stubborn refusal to just go along, to be more like the others, to get over myself.

It was worse than I'd imagined. Not only had the girls waited, but so too had the boys.

And what had my counsellor said, as she'd left to fetch me? How had she accounted for my lengthy delay?

All eyes were on me.

My heart pounded in my ears.

Colours brightened, while outlines smeared.

I might faint. Wouldn't that be the crowning glory?

Someone handed me a bow. His lips moved, but I couldn't hear what he said. My damp hands slipped on the varnished wood.

There is a memory of a brief flash of wistfulness, of thinking this was something I could have enjoyed, if not for the fact that I had to attempt it before a Live Studio Audience.

The rest is blank.

Once fight is ruled out and flight proven unsuccessful, a sort of manic blindness can take over. An out-of-body, out-of-mind blur.

Really, it's a miracle no one was injured, as I let go of the taut, straining bowstring.

Not until lights-out, when I retreated to my musty bunk bed and the dull exhaustion of the post–adrenaline rush, was I able to reflect on the morning's events. My motives and reactions formed a tight and tangled knot which I had no power to unravel. I knew only one thing, and that with a cold, sure certainty: I was a failure—a complete, abject, repetitively offending failure. I acted on instinct, trusted my intuition, and it had all gone horribly wrong. Far from avoiding humiliation, I had only managed to draw attention to my defects. What's more, my actions stripped the occasion of any crumb of pleasure it may have held.

Thing is, while we shy folk may, from time to time, offend or even injure the unsuspecting, happy-go-lucky extrovert, we inflict the most damage on ourselves. I wanted to blame the boisterous boys, the clueless camp counsellors, or my well-intentioned parents. But in the end I only—and always—blamed myself.

What was wrong with me?

Why, when my friends proposed a spur-of-the-moment sleepover, would I instantly start running a ticker-tape of possible excuses through my mind, hoping to find something that would sound plausible, convincing, without giving myself away or hurting someone's feelings? Why, when everyone else delighted in the prospect of a crowded, noisy party, would I feel a flutter of dread upon being invited?

There was no element of conscious decision-making here, no casual "can't be bothered." When faced with social expectations unanticipated or overwhelming, a sensation I can only describe as claustrophobic came over me, making some part of me gasp for air and hunt for the nearest exit. I'm sure I trampled a few toes in my headlong rush for the door; and this only made things worse, as the frustration and shame were overlaid with guilt.

At university, I learned that introverts are not simply shy people with defective social skills, but individuals who need solitude in order to refuel.

This revolutionized my thinking. I was not—at least not only—damaged goods. It wasn't just that there was something wrong with me. I was simply wired a certain way. Different, not worse.

But—if I was merely different, then why could I not be accepted on my own terms? All my life I'd been told, in myriad ways, that my natural tendencies were inappropriate, shameful, and not to be indulged. If I tried to extricate myself from some exhausting social experiment, I was either overridden—"Oh, don't be silly, you'll have fun"—or accused of rudeness, of being a spoilsport. One option would have been to learn to lie well. But mendacity is also wrong, I was told.

So the only alternative was to pretend, to live a lie, rather than tell one.

We frown on most forms of proselytism today. Tolerance is the name of the game—except when it comes to rooting out any whiff of anti-social behaviour. The word "loner" evokes images of Unabombers, psychopaths, addled conspiracy theorists; men obsessed with guns and women who hoard cats.

Extroverts rule the world—or at least, they become camp counsellors, run for student council and plan events—and they consider it a calling to jolly shy people out of their shells. Often they pursue this goal with an evangelical fervour that would make a nineteenth-century missionary blush. But while some shells may be limiting and unhappy, others have become, over time, carefully crafted shelters, designed to provide much-needed breathing space in the midst of the madding crowd.

The fact is, they don't need to be angry.

And we don't need to be fixed.

I recently interviewed a shy young man. He stammered, he blushed, he fidgeted. I found it all rather refreshing, disarming, even, after meeting with some of his overconfident, entitled peers. Clearly, he had not mastered the art of the cover-up. I felt I was glimpsing something real and genuine, something authentic. Not that confidence is always false, or forced, of course. But one thing about shyness is that it's awfully hard to fake convincingly— especially to one of our own.

VIVIAN HANSEN

Fisher Woman

The light altered,
and the coral translucence of the fish
I meant to catch in my barren hands
shifted, to black.
Eluding me.
I want to be a fisher woman;
a fisher of all women.
A Woman who Fishes
without a rod,
taut steel wires,
barbed hooks,
or bait.
If just the look of me
would be enough
to lure the trout
sliding through my hands.
Easy pickings for my table.
But there, the light shifted,
circled, in cold rain and dun cloud.
The sun-drowsy fish
slept and they were changelings
I could not catch.
My nightshirt clung to my breasts,
and there I stood, in wet waking.

The Culture of Shyness

ALEX BOYD

Sacraments of ducked heads and disappearances,
never interrupting a moment with a mobile phone,
renting videos unscathed, evenings dented
by someone's failure to respond, anxious
about asking for salt, unable to eat with someone
looking, arranging books and chairs in cafeterias
to create tents of space, floating in the babble,
making note of the spaces between steps, moments
between events, scattered human anchors
settled into the soil of peace and quiet to consider
progress. Stamped out by drama teachers.

Under the l

*Country Time, Country Time, tastes like that good old-fashioned
lemonade.*

Since it was the seventies, no one complained that we didn't
use real lemons. Good old Country Time lemonade from the
silver canister in my mom's kitchen cupboard was easy to make,
inexpensive, and tasted great.

My best friend Renata took care of sales while I mixed and
poured. Talking to strangers had always been difficult, and I knew
a good portion of the world from between my parents' knees.
Stacking Styrofoam cups into towers on the plastic card table
Renata's mother lent us was an ideal compromise—I felt every
part of a very important business venture, without having to leave
my comfort zone.

Our first customer wore the kind of dark pointy sunglasses I
imagined a criminal would. Though directly facing the sun, he took
them off, looked past Renata and straight at me. Couldn't he see
I was the mixer, the cup stacker, the janitor?

"Good morning, girls." Though he addressed us in the plural,
he spoke to me. "Isn't it a wonderful day for a glass of lemonade?
I sure hope you don't have any real lemons in here. They make
my throat swell something terrible."

"Um, well, it's Country Time lemonade," I answered, praying
the nervous stutter I'd only recently conquered wouldn't start up
again.

"Great." The deep wrinkles around his eyes when he smiled
were inconsistent with his gravelly voice, glasses, and fedora.
"Two cups, please."

As he drank the first cup, a few drops dribbled onto his goatee.

"Merci. That was delicious," he said with a wink, and asked for the second cup to go.

He slowly replaced the glasses on the bridge of his nose and said, "I'll see you girls later."

From behind, his walk and baggy pants reminded me of a circus ringleader. I felt momentarily sad for him, but hoped I wouldn't run into him again.

Our lemonade ran low around mid-afternoon. Our feet hurt from standing, so we sat in the grass near the bandstand. Renata tallied our profits. We were successful—we had earned over twelve dollars. Our coins divided evenly, we wandered toward the beach and the annual Sea Festival.

We each had a six-dollar decision to make. The greasy smell from the hot dog vendors and the popcorn stands tickled the backs of our throats, and reminded us we hadn't eaten since breakfast. The ice cream sundaes at Swensen's and the fresh baked Cookies by George lured us until we set our sights on the most dominant attraction: the red-and-white striped Bingo tent.

We crept around the outskirts of the tent. We figured kids weren't allowed in without an adult, but we were dying to know what kind of prizes the back wall offered, so we peeked in at a spot where the tent flaps overlapped and provided us a glimpse inside.

The array of potential winnings was spectacular: colour televisions, blenders, five-speed bicycles, bocce ball sets, and beach and deck furniture. There was even a record player with a plastic dome top—the kind my friend Kendall had in her room. I fantasized about listening to my two records on it. *Shaun Cassidy* and *The Adventures of Davy Crocket*.

Davy, Davy Crocket, king of the wild frontier.

My parents hadn't yet replaced our black-and-white TV since it had broken the year before, and would be thrilled if I brought home a colour set. The blender would be great, too; Renata's mom had one and made smoothies for her all the time.

We longed to gamble our lemonade fortunes in hopes of winning one of the prizes, but the cigarette smoke from the Bingo players inside formed a forbidding cloud.

We let down the tent flap and were walking across the grass to the popcorn cart when a deep voice boomed over the microphone: "Well, lookie over there! If it isn't the lemonade girls."

We turned around. Though we were outside the tent, the Bingo Master had a clear view and recognized us from behind. "Turn around for a moment girls and give us a wave," his voice coaxed into the microphone.

My bare legs started to shake and my heart pounded so hard the silkscreened kitten on my red T-shirt crawled. It was him. He was the Bingo Master.

"How many of you folks bought lemonade from these girls today? Raise your cups if you did."

A few familiar faces raised their hands.

"How about you girls join us in the Big Top for a game? There are plenty of seats."

I was trapped by the insistence in his words. He had bought our lemonade, so I felt I owed him something in return.

"Over there are two spots between Joyce and Marie." He pointed at two grey-haired women. Renata and I wove our way to the blue picnic bench in the middle and squeezed in. Ashtrays overflowed on tabletops zigzagged with cracks.

A teenage boy in a red-and-white-striped apron brought our cards, and collected the three-dollar playing fee.

"In honour of my very special guests, the 'lemonade girls,' we are going to play Coverall. You need to fill up one entire card." He held up a card and covered it with his gloved hand.

The metal mesh of the bench dug into the backs of my thighs. I felt nauseous and gauged the distance to the porta-potties near the entrance.

"Good luck and let the game begin!" he announced into the microphone.

He turned the handle of the Bingo cage, and the coloured balls popped around inside. The machine reminded me of the hot-air popcorn popper displayed amongst the prizes.

"First square, B-14. B-14, ladies and gentlemen. Do we have a B-14?" Renata and I both had B-14.

"Next square N-32. N-3-2. Does anyone have N-32?" I had N-32. Renata didn't.

"I-29, G-47, O-62," he announced in rapid succession. My heart raced. I quickly filled up my squares. If I won, that would mean actually standing up and shouting "BINGO" in front of all these strangers. But, I wasn't a winner; I never won at anything.

"N-45, B-3, I-20, O-70. Only two more squares to fill and...

"N-40, B-12."

My card looked like a cardboard quilt. No empty squares. My vision blurred and time slowed down. Renata and the elderly woman on my left urged me on. My thighs were itchy and had a red criss-cross pattern on them.

"Um, Bingo?" I cried.

Bingo Master noticed right away. He'd kept his dark glasses on during the entire game, but I felt his eyes were on me.

"We've got a winner over here! I knew when I first saw her that she was born under a lucky star. Come on up, young lady. Show me what you've got."

On rubber legs I wove between the tables to the front. I felt all eyes upon me, and kept my head bent low. He took off his glasses, the way he'd done that morning, and re-read the numbers out loud. I felt the weight of his hands on my shoulders and he turned me toward the wall of prizes. I was to pick anything I wanted.

The tent was silent. In front of all these people, what I chose would define me. I was frozen with fear and wondered what Renata would have picked. I looked at the TV, the blender, the turntable, but I didn't want to appear greedy. I pointed to the first and most easily accessible prize on the lower shelf. A pink, synthetic blanket folded into a clear plastic cover.

"What? That? asked the Bingo Master in an unbelieving tone. "Come on, you must be kidding? He swept his arms across the wall. "Look at the goldmine of winnings! Are you sure you want this blanket?"

I nodded.

"What about the bicycle or the barbeque set?"

I wanted him to leave me alone. I wanted to disappear. Bingo Master's eyes squinted in confusion. He bent down to retrieve the synthetic blanket slowly, as if allowing me time to change my mind.

"You're sure?" he asked.

I wanted to scream at him, "Of course I'm not sure. Of course I don't want this ugly blanket. You're an adult, aren't you supposed to help me? Can't you just pick the bicycle or that great barbeque set for me?"

Instead, I nodded and held out both hands. There was the rush of applause. I averted my eyes as I returned to my seat.

"It's a nice blanket," Renata said with a limp smile, and put her hand on my shoulder. I hung my head and wondered how we'd share it.

The Bingo Master continued calling the letters and numbers, but with seemingly less enthusiasm.

I lived in the shadow of this shyness until well into my adult life.

The night it began to shift was Christmas Eve, a decade ago. I was returning home by train to Osaka where my then-husband and my three-year-old waited. I'd worked a one-night job as a well-paid "Bunny Girl" at a Lions Club convention in Kyoto on what was the holiest night of the year for me. When I got home there was a gift for me from my husband, under our little white Christmas tree. A tube of red lipstick—a shade I'd never wear. I tried it on, and though it was far too bold a colour, it was excellent for writing on the bathroom mirror. "Find my voice," I scrawled at the top, so as not to interfere with daily grooming rituals, but bold enough for me to take notice.

It didn't happen overnight, and a decade later, across an ocean, remarried, raising a teen and a toddler, I still struggle with bouts of insecurity and guilt. But if I won at a Bingo game today, I'd be sure to pick the biggest, baddest prize on the wall.

High School Shyku

LORI D. ROADHOUSE

No, I can't go out.
I'm babysitting that night.
Sorry.

EVE S. KRAKOW

Young Expressions

IT HAPPENS TO EVERYONE at some point: a blast from the past. You run into someone you haven't seen for years, maybe ten, maybe twenty, and you are jolted back to another time, another life.

Hi Eve, it's Sean!

Which Sean? From Young Expressions, of course! I've been trying to find you for ages! I have a stack of your old letters next to me on my computer desk. I see by your profile photo that you have two lovely children. I would love to hear what you're up to these days.

Best wishes,
Sean

P.S. Have you seen the YEP Facebook page? Check it out!

My insides jumped a mile high when I saw that email. Sean. Young Expressions.

Young Expressions, or YEP as we called it back then, was a performing arts group I joined as a teen. The group gave me the chance to act, to sing, and even to write. But it did so much more than that. It was a magical place far, far away from the dinginess of high school. YEP gave me a chance to rid myself of the awkwardness that followed and clung to me like the stench of skunk. YEP was a refuge, a fresh start. Sitting on the carpeted floor that first day at the rehearsal space in an old warehouse, listening to the director as she sat on the floor in front of us talking to us as equals—I sensed this day marked a new beginning.

I met people I never would have come into contact with otherwise: poor kids, rich kids, kids from troubled backgrounds. We put together shows about racism, the nuclear arms race, domestic violence, teen suicide. I spent all my weekends with Young Expressions and then my entire summer. Our rehearsal space felt more like home than my real home. In my last year of high school, I was even chosen to be part of the group's European Tour.

Then I started college, made new friends, and started seeing a guy. Eventually I left YEP behind, like something I'd outgrown. And now, twenty years later, a message.

I visit the YEP Facebook page. I scan the group member names, recognizing about half. I read through some of the posts. People have been listing their "Top 10" memories, mostly funny incidents, the material of inside jokes.

I want to say hello, to reach out to them, to let them know I'm here. But I hesitate. Twenty years.

I hover, observe, unobserved, invisible. Just like back then. But it's different this time—I just want to find the right words. Because once you click "share" your words are there forever. These people don't know me anymore, and I want to leave the right impression. It's so easy to come across as stupid in these posts. I'll post a comment soon. I just need to think about what to say.

In that quiet hour when the kids are finally in bed and the dishes washed, I open my closet, push the clothing aside, and pull out my box of YEP paraphernalia.

I carry the box to the dining room and spread the contents out on the table. There are old programs, pages from show scripts, newspaper clippings. All in black and white, like an old movie. With each item I turn over, memories race back. Here's the program from the first summer festival, glossy pages bursting with expectation. A schedule of the shows, with dates, times, and theatre numbers listed. Part of a play script I'd completely forgotten about. Brittle newspaper clippings about the summer festival. An interview with the director. More scripts, in courier font, held together by staples and paperclips, my notes scribbled in the margins.

I dig further into the box. At the bottom are my two photo albums from the European Tour. I lift them out. They're the old kind; the pages have a sticky background covered by a clear plastic sheet. You peel back the sheet, place your photos, then press the plastic back down, trying to smooth out the wrinkles. I turn the pages slowly. They have yellowed; in one album, the glue has dried and the photos are sliding around. I haven't looked at these albums in a long, long time. The photos are smaller than I remembered. And they're all so blurry. I thought I was a better photographer than that. Or was it the camera? Finally I realize the fuzziness comes from fading. The colours have become washed out; the contrast is gone.

Here's Lulu, posing with puckered red lips in front of the Bulldog bar. Here's Sean, in that faded jean-jacket I loved so much, standing at a bus stop with Brendan and Étienne making "mouth music," as I had titled it (my first encounter with beat-box). Here's Brendan dancing with Solange on the empty stage in Amsterdam. Here's a group shot, taken in front of a chartered bus.

Everyone else in the photos looks so hip, so cool. I look awful. Awkward, ugly. Bulky clothing, long unshaped hair that makes my face long and somehow draws attention to my nose. Huge glasses. Ugh. And funny how I have all these pictures of other people in action, being silly, doing things. That was me: always the observer, the outsider, the anti-participant.

The house is devoid of human sound. The refrigerator hums.

Looking through the clippings, the faded, photocopied pages of typewritten scripts, the photos, I remember. I begin to make a mental list of my own "Top 10" moments. But I'm not ready to post it on Facebook. I don't want to put it out there just yet. I wait. I hover. I hesitate. Just a few keystrokes separating thought from action. Fantasy from reality.

And then I find the diary.

Montreal, October—, 1986

Dear Diary,

We leave tomorrow. We had our final rehearsal this morning. Celia said she was proud of us and gave the usual rah-rah pep talk—not that we needed it, everyone is so excited. Europe, here we come!

I'm excited but anxious. Everyone in the play seems to have bonded but me. I suppose it's my own fault but I have no idea how to change the situation. It's almost as if it's too late. I've built this barrier and the more I think about it, the higher and stronger it gets.

Day One: Amsterdam

What a day. Dad brought me to the airport. Everyone came with their parents, but I was still embarrassed. I don't want to share this world with Dad; he doesn't understand. Once my bags were checked and he saw that I was in good hands, he gave me a hug. "Have a good time, cookie!"

I sat with Étienne on the plane. Étienne has the definition of tousled blond hair that you just want to run your fingers through. He is one of the kindest and gentlest people in the group. A good actor, too. Well, pretty much everyone on the tour can act better than me. I'm still not sure why Celia chose me, but I'm ecstatic and thankful that she did.

When dinner came around in the self-contained packages that are so much fun to open, there was Gouda cheese. Étienne turned to me holding up the packet and said, "Now that's a good-a cheese!" It was a silly pun but it made me happy.

Hisako was terrified of flying and drank tons. We had a choice of red or white wine with our meal, but somehow she snuck into the area where the wine was kept and pocketed several bottles. I've never seen someone so truly terrified of flying. Or so drunk. She threw up in the bathroom as soon as we landed. Lulu got sick on the plane too. I don't know if it was nerves or alcohol. Actually, by the time we arrived at the youth hostel, half the cast was sick.

The hostel is pretty basic. All the girls are in one room and all the guys in another, including the adults with us. But there are twice as many girls, so that's eleven of us in one big room. The room has bunk beds and a big bathroom with common showers and sinks. Everyone keeps complaining about the lack of privacy, but I don't mind. I'm happy to be in the same room as everyone else.

Day Two

Today we put on our first show. It was amazing! Adrenaline was sky high. Sean and Hisako outdid themselves. I was nervous at first, but once we got on stage I was fine. We've rehearsed it so many times I don't think I could go wrong if I tried.

We're staying one week in Amsterdam and one week in Brussels. There's this guy arranging for schools and youth groups to come see us. After each show we go and sit on the front of the stage, our legs dangling down, and the audience asks us questions about the play. Last night Sean fielded a lot of the questions, as did Hisako, Lulu, and Celia, of course. I listened, fascinated at the ease with which they expressed themselves.

A child's cry jolts me back to the present. Like a startled rabbit, I straighten and freeze, straining to hear if one of the kids has woken up. Silence. Maybe Alex was having a bad dream again. I relax but skip ahead in the diary, scanning the entries. Then, a word clutches hold of my stomach.

...this pain in my gut, boring a hole, and it's getting deeper and deeper. I saw Étienne give Lulu a hug this morning and I wanted to cry. Every little incident reminds me that I don't belong, pushes me further into my hole. Now I'm so far down the hole that it seems impossible to climb out. I can't just come down to breakfast one morning and give everybody hugs like Lulu does, and ask brightly, "So what are we doing today?" The relationships and attitudes have been set.

I know I have to talk to somebody. I have even decided who: Sean. He has such an easy time communicating with people, and he always seems to know what to say. His ambition is to be a writer. He's already written a few plays.

But I have no idea how to approach him.

Day Seven
Argh.

Earlier this afternoon I was sitting here on the top bunk writing in this diary. Everyone else was out. There was a knock on the door, and Sean poked his head in. My heart leapt.

"Is Sherri here?" he asked.

"Uh, no. I think she might be downstairs."

"I didn't see her there. I thought she might be up here."

"Oh. Well, I don't know then."

There must be something else I can say, I thought, but didn't know what. He waited a minute at the doorway, almost expectantly, or maybe also trying to think of something else to say.

"Well, see you later, I guess," he said finally.

"Sure."

The moment he shut the door I started kicking myself. Story of my life.

Day Ten: Brussels
Our days are a blur of rehearsals, reworking scenes, making changes. We also seem to spend a lot of time waiting: waiting for people to arrive, or for something technical to be fixed. This morning I wandered through the empty theatre to find Solange and Brendan dancing on stage. They seemed to be having so much fun. There was an obvious sexual tension, too. I asked if I could take a picture of them. They posed for the camera.

Day Eleven
Something really surprising happened yesterday. I was alone in my room, sitting on my bed reading, when Hisako came in. Hisako and I hardly ever speak to each other. She asked me what was wrong.

"Nothing," I said.

She sat down on my bed, picked up my book from my hands and turned it over to see the cover. "You know, sometimes guys are easier to talk to," she said. "You might want to talk to Étienne, or Sean. They're very easygoing."

The book was *Life is Elsewhere*, by Milan Kundera. One of my favourite authors.

"We're all here together," she said. "Sometimes it's good to just walk up to someone and ask for a hug. Anyone here would understand that."

A hug was what I wanted more than anything.

Hisako handed my book back and left the room.

Then this morning, as everyone was filtering into the rehearsal space as usual, Étienne came over and said hi. My insides jumped. I'm surprised anytime anyone starts talking to me. I have no idea what to say or what to do with myself. But then he gave me a hug! Hisako must have said something to him.

Day Twelve
I can't believe the trip is almost over already.

Day Thirteen, very very late
I'm exhausted and using a tiny lamp so as not to wake anyone, so Diary, please excuse the messy handwriting. But I just had to get it all down as soon as I could.

Earlier this evening, when everyone was just hanging out in their rooms, I sauntered into the guys' room, as casually as I could, to join the conversation. Or to listen, anyway. I'm not very good at joining conversations.

Sean was standing in front of the mirror, combing his hair. He was fooling around with some sort of gel. I sat behind him, on his bed. I could see his reflection in the mirror, and my own. There were other people in the cramped room: Brendan, legs hanging over the side of the top bunk, plucking away at a guitar; Étienne, cross-legged on the floor, writing in a notebook. My insides were a thrashing sea. Twisting into a knot. I had decided that I would talk to Sean that night about how I was feeling. If I could just let it out, tell someone what was going on, everything would be better. I wouldn't be alone anymore.

I sat there and watched Sean comb his hair into a peak. He laughed and then decided to try something else. There I was, just inches from him. All I had to say was, "Sean, can I talk to you for a minute?" and it would be out, the ice broken, the barrier brought down, the bottle uncorked. I said the words over and over again in my head. Just those few words, to break through from fantasy to reality. In fact, all I had to do was say his name. Then the spell would be broken. I just had to open my mouth, push the air through my vocal chords, shape the syllables with my lips and tongue. Just one word separated my being trapped inside to my being in the real world. I felt like I was getting ready to jump off the highest diving board I'd ever seen. Nothing had ever seemed so difficult.

I sat there watching his reflection in the mirror. I observed the strands of dark hair parting through the teeth of the comb as he brought it across his head in slow, deliberate strokes. My heart was pounding in my ears. My hands were trembling. I slid them under my thighs and sat on them.

Brendan was humming along with his guitar. He made some comment. Étienne laughed and said something in response. Sean turned his head from side to side, admiring his work.

It was clearly a boys' room: socks, T-shirts and jeans lay in little heaps on the floor, audio-cassettes were scattered about, books and an electric shaver spilled from a knapsack. An orange peel sat on the dresser alongside a dog-eared script. The room had a musty smell, a mix of dirty socks and aftershave.

"Sean."

I heaved it out like a hundred-pound medicine ball.

He looked up at my reflection.

"Can we talk?" I said.

As if he had been expecting this, he nodded, put down his comb, and walked out into the hall where we'd have some privacy. I followed. My face was hot, my legs were shaking. I didn't look at Brendan or Étienne.

We sat on the floor. I took a deep breath.

"I just don't feel part of the group," I began.

He drew his legs up and put his arms around his knees, watching me.

I focussed on a crack between the floor tiles and tried to explain what I was feeling. It wasn't easy, but it was so much easier than I had thought it would be, now that the ice was broken. The words came out in a jumble, not at all as I'd planned.

When I was finished, I kept staring at that crack. The tiles were a discoloured grey, worn from use.

Out of the corner of my eye, I saw Sean stretch his legs again, lean back onto the wall. He told me that several people had noticed that I wasn't comfortable and that I was upset. He told me they all wanted me to feel part of the group.

"You have to let go a bit, take some chances," he said. "If you talk to people, they'll listen. People want to get to know you."

He was silent for a moment, and so I looked up. He seemed to be looking at something far away. Then he told me a story about his sister, something about how she was always needy and took everyone for granted and never knew how to thank people, until one day she wrote him a letter. Thank you, it said. It was the most beautiful letter he'd ever received.

I wasn't exactly sure how this story was supposed to help me. I guess he was saying that some things are hard to do, but you just have to take the risk.

Then he gave me a big hug. I clung to him. I never wanted it to end. I was also afraid that if I let go I'd start crying.

Lulu popped her head out of her room to tell us it was time to get ready—we were all going out that night. So that was it. We stood up and he went back to his room to get changed. But I felt relieved. I realized that nothing was really resolved, but I felt like a big tumour in my gut had been removed. I could breathe a little easier.

I followed Lulu into our room to get dressed. I wasn't sure what to wear. I didn't have anything appropriate.

"Here, try this," Lulu said, digging out a khaki cotton mini-skirt. I put it on over my black tights. It fit well. I'd never worn a mini-skirt before.

"What should I wear with it?" I asked.

She looked through my clothes and pulled out a black acrylic sweater with a wide V-neck.

"Put this on. Wait—turn it around so the V is in back. Yeah, like that. Perfect!" The wide V made the sweater droop slightly off my shoulder, like in the movie *Flashdance*. Then she said, "Would you let me do your hair and makeup?"

It was nice to have someone taking care of me.

Lulu had me bend my head over so that my shoulder-length hair fell completely upside down, and then emptied half a can of hairspray into it. I closed my eyes and tried not to breathe in too much of the chemical smell. I brought my head up again and she sprayed a bit more, making sure my hair kept its volume but stayed out of my face, and teasing strands in front with her fingers.

Then it was makeup time. She pushed aside my black eyeliner and took out her own plum-coloured eyeliner. My eyes watered as I tried to keep them open so that she could apply the liner under my eyes. Then, eye shadow and mascara. "You have such long lashes," she told me. "A lot of girls would kill for eyelashes like yours." Finally, bold, dark red lipstick—Lulu's trademark. The transformation was complete. I looked in the mirror and was very pleased.

When I came out of the room several of the guys whistled. Sean flashed me a big grin.

"Wow. You look fantastic," he said.

I felt my cheeks go red under the blush that Lulu had applied. "Thanks. It's Lulu, really."

"No," he said. "It's you."

At the nightclub, I sat with some of the girls in a row of chairs near the dance floor. Music blared. Bodies moved through the smoke-filled darkness; a strobe light caught their movements in stop and start slow-motion. I hadn't had any alcohol but was feeling the buzz of being all dressed up and out on the town with the gang. I belonged. The new Eve.

I started nodding my head to the music. Lulu noticed and gave me a thumbs-up, and I smiled but stopped moving, self-conscious.

Later, someone—I don't remember who—pulled me to the dance floor. At first I was self-conscious, standing there with the others in the middle of the dance floor, trying to move my feet and hands to the beat, feeling jerky and uncoordinated. I didn't know if it should be looking at the faces of the people near me or past them or at my own hands and feet.

But then I closed my eyes. And, for a few minutes, I began to... let go. I stopped thinking about everyone else. I just let the music wash over me. The beat pulsed through me, making my body sway and my feet light. The music turned into a wispy substance and my arms moved through it, painting colours in the air. I was weightless. Only the music and the dancing existed.

Then my arm made contact with other flesh. I stopped and opened my eyes. I'd bumped into another girl. She hadn't even noticed and was still dancing. I tried to re-enter my trance but felt ridiculous, so after a few jerky movements I went back to sitting on the sidelines.

Still, I feel that tonight was the beginning of something. Something good.

Day Fourteen

This afternoon was our last show. When it was finished and the stage went to black, we all stood there for a moment, not wanting to move. Later we all went for dinner. There was lots of reminiscing about the last two weeks, lots of laughing. Lulu and Hisako cried.

I'm really going to miss everyone. I can't stand to think about it.

Day Fifteen, on the plane

Sean came into my room while I was packing last night. He took my hands and said, "We've got a lot to learn from each other. This is just the first chapter." Then he gave me a big hug.

I've come to a decision: I am going to change. I've got to. I've got to start showing my feelings more and telling people what I think. It's going to be hard, but I am tired of being trapped inside myself. I am tired of always being on the sidelines. I have got to start taking chances. A few days ago I didn't think I had the strength, but since my conversation with Sean and the night out with the gang, I feel like it's possible. I can do it if I really try.

Anything is possible.

I put down the diary. I close my eyes, digging my palms into my eye sockets.

My life now is Aviva, two and a half, soft blonde curls, a warm little face that comes right up to mine and plants tiny wet kisses on my cheek. She holds my head in her two tiny hands, we rub noses and she giggles. She is mature, determined, assertive: she stands with her hands on her hips, brow furrowed, declarative. Always chattering away, the social butterfly, joining in other children's games.

My life now is Alex, shy, moody, sensitive like his parents. One minute all boy, running through the house with his toy high-speed train flying on invisible tracks in the air, jumping on the sofa, making silly faces; the next, the studious five-year-old, amazing me with his probing questions and keen leaps of logic.

I think of my husband. Protective, caring. Quick-witted, a problem solver, a doer. But also a romantic and a dreamer. Affected inside by the world without, but not wanting to show it.

And me? Different from twenty years ago, to be sure: engaging with people, with life, more of a participant. But still...there are moments. Moments when I realize I've missed a social cue. Moments when the wall goes up again. And those moments are not so few or far between.

I open my eyes, stand up, and wander into the living room. The Lego has been pushed into a neat pile in the middle of the carpet, a half-built spaceship waiting for morning. I run my fingers across the spines of the books lining the shelves—novels, short-story collections. Dictionaries for my translation work, thesauruses, style manuals. Of course they're all available electronically now, but sometimes I want the physical connection of feeling the pages between my fingertips, flipping ahead too far and then having to turn back, or maybe reading the adjacent entries. Rows of magazines, boxes of newspaper clippings, some of them my own. A literary journal containing one of my short stories.

A truck rumbles by outside. I glance out at the leaves of the birch tree, outlined by the streetlight, and I move to open the window. Cool air rushes in over my skin. I close my eyes. The night air caresses my cheeks, my forehead, my neck. Soothing. Reassuring.

Back in the dining room, I turn on my laptop. I open Facebook and stare at the screen for a few seconds. Then I start to type.

Author's note: names in this story have been changed.

My Dear X*

ELIZABETH ZOTOVA

THIS LETTER is meant to convey to you the extent to which my adoration reaches. This shall, too, be an outlet for my mind (through which I hope you may come to comprehend me better). Though at the current time, I've no qualms about our relationship, I do fear that some problems (minute and insignificant as they may be) could fester. Such a misfortune could ultimately be destructive—thus, I shall divulge upon the matters momentarily.

Please refrain from assuming this is meant to upgrade your understanding of me—the level you've bothered reaching is not only satisfactory, but quite admirable. Alas, I must continue this thought, and add, "save upon two matters."

I believe you have guessed that, primarily, there's the issue of my eating habits. I do, in fact, eat. I've made a habit of surviving, apparently. You must drop all ideas that my consumption is irregular or insufficient. Darling, I adore you, but to say that it "doesn't matter that I don't look emaciated," and can still be "starving myself" is madness. If this ridiculous notion were to abandon your brilliant mind, it would, no doubt, become more lustrous.

Moving on, now, into the very framework of my being, I come to what you've labelled as the lesser problem. Indeed, regretfully, the problem is me. The word used to describe my illogical malady is one which causes a great anger to rise up in me, and consume me from inside—"shy." Three letters, one syllable, a meaning unfit for describing me, and so extraordinarily quickly capable of evoking sadism.

Initially, I was shocked by the disdain which would be shown by grade school teachers, for not being obnoxious, and eager to flaunt stupidity. To think—whole classrooms of blatantly idiotic imbeciles were constantly praised for their lack of self-restraint, while I was reprimanded for my reserve.

Eventually, I began to notice that everyone takes you for an idiot until they see some sort of proof. For me, this has always come in the form of writing—as willingly speaking has never been my strong point. I do agree with assuming everyone's pretty dim until I obtain contrary evidence. In no way, however, do I uphold the belief which society largely holds—that reserve and preference not to speak constantly and pointlessly should automatically be seen as a flaw.

While I know that, at times, this particular quality of mine causes you mild discomfort, please try to understand that it is absolutely entrenched in me. If I've nothing to say, I'll just as well choose to say nothing at all. There are three possibilities for my keeping quiet: I have nothing relevant to add; I feel out of place; I feel the company is not worth wasting words upon.

You should really try to see it from my point of view. I don't know how I could stand it if you couldn't, and just kept pushing me, and trying to nurture some sort of social side. You'll just keep getting upset every time you fail. I am not one who can easily speak of even trivial things, if it's with people to whom I've not become accustomed. The first month around you, my posture, never mind the conversational aspect, constantly ravaged my mind. A perfectionist I cannot call myself—that's an unattainable goal. I think I just want to be liked by the few with whom I care to maintain relationships. As the number is low, the quality of the few cannot be compromised by misperceptions.

It's not that I get flustered, exactly, around others. But I am often left disappointed with my replies, and then lie in bed with a ton of improved and revised answers. Perhaps there is something not quite right with that. My will to please isn't all that strong. Rather, it is proving to myself that I have self-worth that is what drives me to act this way.

However, since this letter is only supposed to be a small window, I shall leave off going further. I chose to write this because it is the way I can truly express myself. Do not hesitate to question me with regard to any of this content. Please don't think I am refusing to change because I am stubborn. I can promise to try (at times) to stray from my convictions. I only ask that you try, as best as you can manage, to see this in a light similar to mine.

Liz

* This letter was written to my long-suffering high-school boyfriend. The relationship marked my first attempt at addressing what I'd long known was an issue in my life: my shyness. Since grade school, I was the kid that couldn't (or wouldn't) "work well with others," or "participate" in class. Reading over this, I can see my sixteen-year-old self certainly seemed concerned with how others viewed her—whether she could admit it or not. I guess, seven years later, it's still hard.

It's difficult to pick apart your own personality. When shyness is part of who you are, it's natural enough to be defensive. It becomes convenient to paint up your argument by telling yourself you don't need other people, and that you're preserving something (like a special secret). The trouble is, before you know it, you've withdrawn into yourself so far, you don't know what's what.

Here's my take on the root of the problem: the shy are bombarded with shame so that they will "hopefully" decide to resist their intro-version. Those deemed successful in this endeavour end up like blind little moths in the sunshine, half-heartedly competing with (to be quite trite) all the iridescent social butterflies of the world. We're rendered, ironically, less functional by society's well-meaning stereo-type of the social cripple.

A real community needs to accept all sorts of people. We're not exactly scene-stealers, so you don't hear much from us shy folk—and that's usually how we like it. But if you did, you'd know that "people-person," "outgoing," and "go-getter" make us cringe. We don't covet those badges. Frankly, if we had it our way, we'd ask, why not reform the loud, the obnoxious? Or at least get them to shut it for just a little bit.

Society's a rat trap, and those who don't participate in obvious ways need to stop being punished. How crass it is that subtlety need be a sin.

BRUCE MEYER

Change
Room

An adolescent's greatest fear
is being the last one to mature.
A smooth body is not a man's.
Power issues from raging glands.

We were hot, salty to the core,
ordered after gym to shower.
The boy who stripped next to me
had grown long, broad and hairy.

Slowly, I removed my cup,
my socks, T-shirt, and stood up.
Naked bums formed a line
and agony boiled beneath my skin.

The tougher ones with shoulder curls
reminded me of imagined girls;
and fleshy backs soft as mine
shed snows of soap around the drain.

Change and nakedness were raw
as my pathetic shape they saw,
while joking, echoed off a shower head,
left my manhood there for dead.

Cloak of Invisibility

MADELAINE WONG

JOSTLING BODIES crammed dimly lit hallways. I had dreaded
my first day of high school, and reality was more terrible than my
fearful imagination. Boys towered over me. No, those weren't
boys. They were giants, with facial hair! Their booming voices
echoed in the cavernous halls. The hulking creatures laughed
and shoved each other while I dodged out of the way. They could
have crushed me beneath the heels of their enormous feet if
they had so chosen. I was at their mercy. For protection, I put on
my cloak of invisibility. With my eyes downcast and my binder
pressed against my chest, I maneuvered through the thick crowd
of adolescent madness. My straight, mousy brown hair hung
lifelessly around my shoulders. My face had recently erupted
in a new crop of bright red zits. I wondered if I had a bad smell
coming from my armpits. I was lucky. The cloak was effective.
The boys had not sensed my presence.

But as scary as the boys were, the girls were more terrifying.
A little further on my quest to find my locker, I came upon
them—the Keres. My blood froze in my veins. They were the
evil spirits released from Pandora's chest, whose purpose was
to create havoc on the Earth. They craved blood, feasting upon
it after ripping the soul free and sending it to Hades. Those
fearsome dogs of the underworld disguised themselves with
too much makeup and, like a pack of yappy, pampered poodles
in bright dress-up clothes, they giggled and simpered their way
to their lockers. Their curly hair bounced as they sang, "Gonna
dance with my baby till the night is through. On Saturday night,
Saturday night. Tell her all the little things I'm gonna do...." My
dowdy self shrank in their presence. They were strong, and my
invisibility cloak fell away. They spotted me, looked me up and

down, taking in my dull appearance. Their upper lips curled in distaste, like they smelled something foul. Then, from the mouth of the alpha bitch, came the dreaded word—"Loser." I felt my soul rip away. I was in Hell, branded, my fate sealed. It was the label from which no teenager could recover.

What was that paralysis, that veil of insecurity that hung between me and others? I could see through it, but it was impenetrable. I was left on the edge, as an observer, not a participant. I stood drowning in a murky puddle of fear and uncertainty, a victim of my own self-consciousness. I couldn't understand why I was treated badly. The frustration and shame were almost too much to bear.

I remembered my mother's words: "Be brave. You need to break out of your shell. Speak up. Once they see what a nice girl you are, they'll want to be your friend." What Mother didn't know was that nice girls were eaten alive.

I had no idea how to start a conversation. What if they didn't want to talk to me? What if I said something stupid? I cared only for self-preservation, couldn't bear the contemptuous sneers, so I kept silent.

High school was a cruel place for the shy introvert. The ability to quietly contemplate was not a skill valued by the general population. It was a place for loud, obnoxious attention-grabbers who were able to walk that thin line, to stand out and to fit in at the same time. I didn't want to be like them. Their inane conversations involving boys, drinking, parties, and smoking dope I found artificial and irritating. I had little interest in those sorts of activities. I was a sensitive child in an insensitive world, my quiet voice muffled by swaggering loudmouths.

I simply wanted to be accepted, and I cared deeply about what other people thought of me. The days passed, and I increasingly felt judged and looked down upon. As a result, my feelings of unworthiness increased.

Hang with a loser and you become one. That is an unwritten rule of high school. For the loser it meant only one thing—a further fall, to the lowest rung on the ladder. It was the worst of all fates.

Woe to that unfortunate soul who became a loner. Even the geekiest, strangest, thickest-eyeglass-wearing boy in the school had a friend. But by the time I entered grade eleven, I had been shunned.

I no longer needed anybody to tell me I was a loser. I felt it deep in my bones, and I beat myself up on a daily basis. "What is wrong with me?" I wondered if it was possible to rid myself of the affliction of shyness, or if I would have to go through life as a bumbling, stammering, despairing, mass of uncertainty. "Is it possible to change?" I longed to become a different person but had no idea how such a thing could be accomplished. I prayed for help, to be released from Hell.

The chance came to me by accident, by a twist of fate, or through the grace of God. Call it what you will. I needed an after-school activity, something suitable for one such as me, who did not get invitations to parties, who did not participate in sports, and who had negligible social skills. I took a pottery class. One day, as I prepared for class, I found I had no clean shirt to wear. Desperate, I entered my big brother's bedroom and opened the bottom drawer of his dresser. Beneath the assortment of underwear and mismatched socks, I found a clean T-shirt. Alleluia! It was plain white with a picture of some sort of plant on the front. Good enough.

I boarded the bus and made my way to the SAIT campus where the pottery class was held. I took my usual spot and began to work my clay—pounding, kneading, and shaping. The process was satisfying, creative, but also physical. As my pot took shape, I glanced up and saw that a boy was looking at me, and smiling. He nudged his friends and pointed in my direction. I avoided eye contact. *Ignore them long enough and they'll go away* was my motto.

At lunch break, I lined up to wash my hands. The boy and his friends stood beside me and invited me to eat with them. I agreed, smiling weakly. "Where should we eat?" they asked me. I shook my head in disbelief. They wanted me to pick the place.

I suggested a place outside, on the grass, in the shade. They followed behind me.

We sat and talked. "Where do you go to school? Want to hang out after?" they asked.

They were interested in me. They laughed when I said something mildly amusing. The boy blushed when I talked to him. The girls copied my mannerisms. I became their paladin. I strolled across the campus with my gaggle of eager minions trailing behind me. I was in my glory.

What was that strange feeling that rose from my chest, which made me want to smile, to hold my head up high, to walk with a determined air? Could it be confidence? What happened that day to make it different from all other days? I contemplated that question on the bus ride home.

I walked in the door that evening and saw my brother's shocked expression. "Why are you wearing that shirt? Take it off before Mom sees."

"Why?" my naive self inquired.

"Because, you idiot, that's a picture of a marijuana plant on the front. If she sees you wearing that she'll kill both of us."

I looked down and it all made sense. I laughed at the absurdity of the situation. For one day I had become a rebel, a bad girl, and all without taking a single toke on a joint. I had found my armour, my golden fleece, and I could now enter the Land of Cool. I didn't have to change who I was, merely how people perceived me. I began to see myself as something other than a pimply-faced, friendless nerd. The girl I saw in the mirror slowly transformed. I learned how to use makeup and a curling iron. As time passed, I learned to hold my head up high and came to understand that I must accept myself before I can expect others to do the same. I then made it clear to the Keres that I would no longer take their abuse. I uttered the magic incantation—a well-formed sentence filled with colourful expletives, combined with a long stare-down. They never bothered me again. I was then able to retrieve my soul and my dignity.

School cliques are near to impossible to break into when one is branded, so I made a decision. I boarded my Argus and set sail on the unknown seas. I started again at another school. My wish was not to be popular, but simply to be accepted, and that is exactly what happened.

⋮ Several decades have passed since those events occurred, and I occasionally meet people from my first high school. Most never knew that I left. I guess I really was invisible. It surprised me to learn that outgoing people struggled with the same uncertainty and fears I did. Some continue to delude themselves, covering their inadequacies with cloaks of bravado. I threw away my protection, my cloak of invisibility, long ago. I no longer need it, nor want it.

SYDNEY SHARPE

Shy and I

WHY

There's always a corner where the shadows of shyness overrun reason. The heart races as it searches for a space as benign as a yogi's retreat; where slow deep breaths bring solace, and the armour of cheer slowly recedes into reflection. Calm and even grace brace the body for the next venture out.

Secluded and content, the racing stops. Shyness eases when the doors are closed and all is contained within. Shyness searches for reasons to stay and never bends to the beyond, even as it beckons repeatedly. But the door to the outside demands to be opened.

SHY

It's so easy for shy to stay inside. The known is contained within a womb where walls of warmth provide all. Outside, the trees are swaying and offering a limb to climb on. The cirrus clouds brighten with the day and then blast off, leaving wanderlust in their wake. It's time to follow the sky, to see but to blend in. Oh, to become the wings of the hummingbird, flapping so fast that motion is momentary. The tiny bird nestles in life's nectar, unseen as it sips and then absconds to the next veiled banquet.

The armour is carefully assembled. Even the clothes convey shadows as shades of black tempt the shy side of the moon. A scarf of many colours conquers the cloak of invisibility. Why not ride the rainbow, every day jumping into the glow of a new colour? Maybe its radiance will release its own invincibility.

The silent mouth suddenly opens, shielded with lipstick that locks in place. It will pull the voice from within. The eyes rest as they see just what they want until they venture forth, on guard.

Lashes, no longer invisible, carry two coats of black for extra protection. It is not enough. Glasses become the safety net for eyes that betray too much. Stroke the hair that is carefully grown, cut, highlighted or lowlighted to catch the sun, but not any notice, as it quietly falls over half the face. Shy hears and sees but is only partly visible—in the mind—and that is all that matters as shy closes the door behind you.

All that is left is shy and you who become two. Listen to the mind as it tells shy what to do until two takes over. The smile moves from within and frees the face to break with the armour. The smile calms and creates the will to play.

Shy jostles with the nerves as it picks a place to join. Shy grabs an outstretched limb and settles on. Ready to wrestle with circumstance, shy succumbs to words that want to win. Yes, energy is contagious especially amongst friends, where the will to exchange and participate propels shy to release the bolt of doubt. Contact is composed, even serene, but never secure.

Don't trust tranquility, because it can dissolve like a clash of egos fighting for centre stage. Oh, to hide from this performance especially when called on to play. Just smile and step away, all the while looking for a door to dart through and quickly close. The escape is complete, and shy emerges to consider another day.

Even with an armour of grace, shy and I are one, sometimes two. We—I and shy—settle in for the long haul, sometimes sinking into the stomach so it bends to the swiftly flowing river of fear. As it ebbs, shy and I part ways, if only in our dreams.

Does shy lack courage? Does shy mask sloth? Does shy get a pass until tomorrow never comes? That way, the cure can't confront the excuse. Maybe it's time to tackle shy head-on, to try and mend, perhaps to end. Look in the mirror of the mind and not turn away. Let's grab two and shy to make I. I will. I do. Every day shy makes the vow to create and conquer the rubber door that too easily bounces off the will to leave.

Shy—I—assemble every thread of strength to knit a sweater so bold that fear takes a pass. And add it to the wardrobe of deception that's always in season but never on sale.

ARITHA VAN HERK

Shades and Shyness

SOMETIMES I SCAN THE INTERNET for mentions of shy
people in history or of prominent shy people still living. Why? To
comfort myself? To alleviate my own reticence? I can't be certain.
I wonder why such lists proliferate. Idle consolation for other shy
people, reassurance that we can all overcome being tongue-tied
and awkward? Or a prurient interest in those beyond our reach,
somehow removed from our regard and thus more intensely the
objects of our interest?

   The directory of those noted for shyness or introversion is
fascinating, not for the people themselves but for what with-
drawal performs. Bertie, otherwise known as King George the VI,
his isolation exacerbated by his stutter. Andrew Warhola, who
became Andy Warhol and impossible to define, shy because he
could not be, prohibited from retreat. Aretha Franklin, introverted
but full of voice. Lawrence of Arabia, the illegitimate child of an
illegitimate child, fatally injured when he swerved to avoid two
boys on bicycles, lost control and was thrown over the handlebars
of his Brough Superior SS100 motorcycle. (The neurosurgeon
attending Lawrence's death began an intensive study of head
injuries and motorcycle riders; his research led to the use of
crash helmets, protective headwear useful to hide behind.) Rita
Hayworth, depressive as well as shy, succumbing to bad husbands
and, finally, Alzheimer's disease, probably because she wanted to
forget the husbands. Joyce Carol Oates, whose still small centre
is offset by the dynamo that produces her novels and short
stories. Emily Dickinson, even her poems bashful, so brief and
elliptical, full of withholding. Albert Einstein, shyer than any equa-
tion. Edgar Allan Poe, tormented by his imagination, the very
pennies left on his grave reclusive. Lucille Ball, despite or

because of her exuberant laughter. Eleanor Roosevelt, determined to live up to her own plainness. Glenn Gould, whose control and intimacy trumped theatricality, an architecture of precision. Greta Garbo, who wanted not only to be alone but to be left alone, who went from a shy soap-lather girl in a barbershop to a woman wearing oversize sunglasses on the streets of New York, part of her elusive mystique her resistance to garrulousness. J.D. Salinger, practitioner of charismatic glossolalia, a man for whom writing was a pleasure but the publication of that writing an interruption. Bob Dylan, the changeable troubadour, reclusive as folk itself, manifestly uncomfortable. Barbra Streisand, fearful of perfection's reach. And Robert De Niro, donning and shucking character parts, his evasive eyes refusing to accede, every performance a detour from shyness.

And me, not at all famous or important, a consummate deceiver.

I am shy. Not painfully shy, but oxymoronically so, like a puzzling conjunction, meticulously dishevelled or subtly exaggerated.

I am shy but I am not inhibited. I am not phobic. I often avert my eyes, but I don't stare at my shoes when I speak. I do not suffer from "social anxiety disorder." (Can any further disorders adorn the necks of ordinary people and their characters?) If I were to be diagnosed, some expert would probably categorize me as a "shy extrovert," someone who performs well (or seems to) externally, but who experiences even in the midst of a talk or a performance (and I do plenty of those), painful thoughts and feelings.

⋮ I cover my shyness well, with the expertise born of years of practice. I can face a lecture hall, I know how to look confident and engaged, but inside, I am curled in a nautilus of—not fear or loathing or terror—just shyness, an ineffable combination of diffidence, reticence, and privacy that is mine alone. Perhaps one reason I don't seem shy is that I want to protect my shyness from people, especially those quick to make judgements and pronouncements, who insist on telling me what and how and who I am, who are quick to assess, quick to dismiss, and even quicker to condemn. My shyness is the secret I hold close, insulate from harm.

My character traits overlap shyness. I am overly helpful because I am shy. I try too hard to include people, to make them feel comfortable, because I am shy. And I abhor hurting people's feelings. I will resort to lies in order to avoid conflict. Of course, because of these chameleonic tendencies, I am often misread, and people feel compelled to give me stick, to misinterpret my hermitic container.

Shyness is a condition that people misunderstand. In a time of glib essentialism, we have come to believe that shyness means silence, modesty, negation. We've been told that shy people are incapable, inarticulate. I am neither, and I appear to be the opposite: capable, articulate, and confident. I am not silent or modest or even self-effacing; I speak well, I know my own abilities, and I will step up to the microphone or the podium with some tremor, but an overall ability to handle the moment.

I resist the tendency to pathologize or to psychologize every trait I possess; it's a cheap way to live, when it seems to me better to simply deal with the characteristics I have acquired, by both inheritance and experience.

I can trace this reserve to the footprint of being a child of immigrants. I have been, my entire life, shy about my background, my family story, my compressed and always inadequate skill, training and achievement. Some would tell me that I suffer from imposter syndrome, an inability to trust my own competence; but unlike the incompetent, who usually do not recognize their own incompetence, I know that I am capable, even accomplished. Occasionally, I surprise myself.

But the indelible ink of origins watermarks every person. I map my shyness back to my childhood and a time when I developed my wide-eyed and irritating curiosity. Growing up in a rural community, seeing only a few people besides my family, meant that outsiders and visitors were to me strange creatures, exotic acrobats. I watched them unobtrusively, from corners or behind doors, recording their words and actions, gathering up every strand of information that I could. Knowing silent children are usually ignored, I stared and stared, curiosity coded by observational intensity, my scrutiny like the glare of a headlamp. If spoken to, I fled. I learned looking, the human trait that has enabled our species to survive in desperate situations. I wanted to know everything I could decipher about the world, but in the process of all I was accumulating, I did not want to reveal my own gaze, and I did not want the world to look at me. In the confused and shifting confines of my youth, with immigrant parents straddling their own transformation from European to Canadian, their own trade-off of languages and customs, I could not imagine who I was. I had to figure out humans and where I belonged in relation to them by watching carefully, by staring hard. Those early encounters shaped my practice as a writer, that of an observer, vigilant but separate, self-contained. And there resides the kernel of my insistent shyness. I notice, pay attention. But I prefer not to be watched or noticed. I want to be invisible.

The off-side of coming from a family trying to figure out the rules of a strange culture and a strange language, the inscrutable manners of Western Canada, was that expected graces, phrases, and mores were mysterious, difficult to access. That this is a common lacuna for immigrants is so obvious as to be redundant. We assume that newcomers want to "assimilate," but learning to re-shape the face into an expression suitable to an alien and mysterious culture is never easy. And while my immigrant parents and siblings had a strong sense of who they had been before their migration, which seemed to give them courage in adapting to this new place, I felt for most of my childhood utterly baffled. Where we were, the rolling parkland of Alberta, was physically specific, but who we were and who I was sounded a different reverberation. Even as I turned that question over and over, a meditation on active participation in the world, I was mystified.

People's secrets reveal themselves when they do not know they are being watched. As a determined watcher, I knew I could discover privacies just so long as I retained my own. I was learning to be a writer; I was also learning how to use shyness to advantage. There is nothing shrewd about this combination of gifts and liabilities—the gaze was my way of remembering every word and gesture. It became and still is my research method, how I gather material. Once I started school, I learned to stare less overtly, but I kept watching, my look sometimes earning me the enmity of those who caught me in the act. My attention is both a trait of the shy and a declaration, a means of constructing a story. As a practitioner of Hazlett's observation that "Reading, study, silence, thought are a bad introduction to loquacity," my education as a writer cemented my shyness early.

I know that I shouldn't be shy. When my first novel was accepted, Leonard Cohen witnessed my contract.

The night before McClelland and Stewart planned to announce that *Judith* had won the Seal First Novel Award, I was told to present myself at a suite in the hotel in Montreal where I had been accommodated. I was 23 years old, utterly naive, as only a homegrown Albertan can be, and shyer than a lost glove. I had no idea of what I was in for, the whole wild publicity ride that the Seal Award would engender, but I had a gut feeling I was going to be buffeted around a bit, and on top of my innate shyness, I was nervous. I was right about the unpredictable experience—I couldn't have been less prepared. When I walked into that hotel suite, I encountered a phalanx of serious men in suits, all executives from the different international publishers who had together contributed to the Seal First Novel Award. There were two disruptions in this rather formidable room, a beautiful Anna Porter and a man I'd met in university. I took a deep breath and focussed on them; they would help me to negotiate this introductory scrutiny. The legendary Canadian publisher Jack McClelland, charming, effervescent, took me around the room and introduced me. "Let me introduce you to—" and "This is—." I remember only a few of the names. "This is Anna Porter." I was made tongue-tied by Anna Porter's unruffled elegance, her kindness. And then came the man I was sure that I had met in university, that I must have taken a class with. "And this," said McClelland, rather like a magician pulling a rabbit out of a hat, "is Leonard Cohen."

If I had been shy before, at that point I almost melted into the floor. Here was the iconic figure of Canadian literature, smiling at me with a gentle beneficence that I could hardly credit. The purpose of that meeting was to ensure that I signed the contract before the press conference and announcement the next day; and yes, Leonard Cohen witnessed my contract. I was knotted with shyness, my eyes following the cursive of his long-fingered hand, a hand that I surely wanted to touch but was prevented from touching by a terrible self-consciousness. He understood, I like to think, offering me the reassurance of his familiarity as an aid to courage for the appraisal I was facing. We both understood that we were the shy ones at some orgy of identification, a trial to our shared self-effacement.

As my writing years progressed, there developed a deeper reason for this diffidence, the collision of private and public person and the magnetism of revenge that seems to attract itself to public figures. When you are a young woman, with early success, you earn, entirely without meaning to, currents of enmity. Like the writer who informed me, with no small hostility, despite the conversation's happening twenty years after the Seal Award, that he had quit his job to write a novel that was supposed to win, and I had stolen the prize. Or like the man who came to a reading, sat in the front row and glared at me throughout, without blinking, then came up and informed me that his wife had left him because she had read one of my novels. One is helpless before such charges; there is nothing to say. Shyness becomes a shield, an escutcheon.

In 1987, I was asked by the Writers' Guild of Alberta to serve as the writer/editor in residence at the annual Strawberry Creek retreat. One beautiful evening, a group of us were going for a walk, when I stepped from the porch into a concealed hole in the uneven ground and turned my ankle. The injury was sudden and serious. Orthopedists later determined that I had torn a ligament, but all I knew at that moment was excruciating pain, pain that literally had me crying and rolling on the ground. While several of the writers tried to help, one of them—and I do not remember who—ran into the lodge and came out with a camera in order to take a picture of me. With shameless glee, she announced that she was never likely to see me in that vulnerable state again. No wonder I am shy; when I am caught off-guard, someone is eager to exploit my exposure. Better to be inscrutable, to look unassailable, to conceal the tight bindings of hurt.

So yes, I wear a disguise, a disguise tough and forthright that does not compromise my inner bashfulness. Yes, I feel empathy, too much empathy, and I know it can trap me, mislead me, woo me into giving to other humans more than I should, pieces of myself that are better withheld. My duality hugs a dark shadow. I want to be gentle and understanding, and so I suffer the psychomorph's dilemma, where I am all things to all around me, and underneath retain a raging shyness that wants to be anything but who I am and anywhere but where I am.

⋮ No matter what the analysts and their cohorts say, shyness is not a social anxiety. Shyness is not the same as stage fright. Shyness is not introversion. Shyness is not a synonym for awkward and does not equate to alienation. Shyness is a quiet place where we resist the lure of glib connection, facile communication, and the whole gaudy circus of humans competing for attention. I would argue that not enough people are selfconscious. And while I do not recommend feeling skittish, fearful, or mistrustful, caution, reverie, and melancholy are allies for the observant writer.

All communication is tactile; the shy person is one who is nervous about touch, that unexpected fracturing of the barrier between one human and another. We live in an age when the body is a self-contained entity, and to interrupt that force field is an act so bold it is almost breathtaking. Why are painful and shy connected? My shyness is not painful but a refuge, an inner ear, a still small centre that keeps me balanced.

Wariness too is underrated. The shy person does not want to tell you all her secrets. And if the shy are considered romantic, trustworthy, a bit plain, then let that designation stand. There is a secret world of shy: luminous, scant, light of foot, and graceful with silence, even strolling arm in arm with irony. Wine can be shy, although food is never allowed to be shy; and clothing should not aspire to be shy but demure. There are days when the sky itself has the shy, naked air of a face just washed of tears.

Does grief exacerbate shyness? Is shyness a stay against chaos and surprise? The complexity of loss hovers here: every word we utter, every gesture we make, will vanish. In this age where all is ephemeral, fast-moving, and disposable, shyness and its withholding articulate the ceremonial, more formal side of engagement.

And so we practise our disguise, we shy extroverts. Blushing occasionally, we retreat behind our masks, the inviolable public personae we've constructed. We over-compensate, faux extroverts who work hard to cover what others invariably read as arrogance or unfriendliness. Umbrella people, we play gregarious so we will not be thought cryptic, reserved, impenetrable, stiff, arrogant, old-fashioned, standoffish, and silent.

I deploy protective coloration to conceal the fact that I am a terribly shy woman who would rather find myself alone in a room with a big-bellied chair and a good book than at a party filled with dazzling people. I'm more brooding owl than peacock. I'm a coyote in an urban park, lurking and alert. Still, I am no Blue Hamlet (a rare tropical fish that prefers to "hide among rock work or hover near the substrate") or Shy Wallflower (*Erysimum inconspicuum*, an uncommon plant with pale yellow flowers, native to Alberta). My awkwardness partners with reticence in the dance of self-possession. And so I hold my shyness, collaborator and doppelgänger, close.

ELIZABETH GREENE

Secret Self

At ten, eleven, twelve, I carried her inside me,
close under my skin, like the blue layer under
grey outer eucalyptus bark.
                              I wrote.
She could jump and touch her toes, dive
from the high tower, laugh at parties
while I, left to myself, would lurk
at the edges, silent oyster, unsure if
it was safe to open.
                        She was the first
woman in Space Academy; I wrote her adventures.

She got me to Chile, said *Yes, let's go!*
I huddled, neck-cramped,
through the dark twelve-hour flight,
less space than you'd give a corpse,
and not horizontal,
without screaming or throwing
my omelette at the snarky stewardess.

I drink in the astringent smells,
pine, eucalyptus, commune with the fig
matriarch with ripening fruit and shiny leaves,
coat more luxurious than mink, ten times as green.

She scrapes the bark and smells, thinks,
healing, sweet. Picks one. Eats.

I'm the one who wants to be the tree.

Disturbing the Universe

Do I dare
Disturb the universe?
            —T.S. ELIOT "The Love Song of J. Alfred Prufrock"

Panic at the party.
All those people animated, assured.
I can no more speak to them than plunge
off a cliff. I gulp,
afraid of inflicting boredom,
bristle silence,
like I'm watching a movie
I can't step into.

I'm paralyzed behind
a wall, transparent, frozen, glass.

I know I'm all inner—
stressed, I curl inside,
watch but don't talk,
try to become invisible
and succeed fairly well.

It's in my horoscope,
all my planets below the horizon,
a complex inner life
that never quits,
but it's hard to throw my thoughts
out into the world.

When I'm home,
or with a friend, or two,
or with a cat,
I uncurl
like a Chinese waterflower,
find my voice,
know, if I want, I can
disturb the universe.

On Mingling

JENNIFER HOULE

After William Meredith

I do what's in character, I look for places
to interrupt you in your small talk
with a well-timed witty remark, or I look
for a place to sit down somewhere
with a book, or I find a plant to consider
and fuss the dry leaves from. I love
to do this, in any case. So it's honest,
and it is so rarely that I find any need
to interrupt; and more rarely still that I should
start a conversation we couldn't finish
given the small time, and the smallness
of our relation. Apertures are increasingly rare,
you know, although—it isn't so much
that they're expensive. It's where

could they go? You don't see screen doors
the way you used to, all the time. We want
sliding doors to all our balconies.
French doors. Double doors into
all the businesses. And maybe double doors
have led to the demise of chivalry—somebody
said that, once, to me, after the strangest
tussle in a vestibule. And I thought yes!
but have they bred a better reciprocity?
We did not agree, but married. Marriage
cannot be the fear? Its specter why
we are the way we are in the crowded rooms

we have bothered to enter, heads on
straight, and feeling hopeful? Screens

at the windows, see, but windows—
anyway, not what I really meant by
apertures. I was thinking more of the voids
we sometimes seem on hand to fill
so squarely it smacks of the fictive.
Too often, I stand on the outer edge
of a close-knit circle doing its philosophy
in self-correcting circles, like it does.
And, though I would like to trigger
a spiral, I stop, mid-wave, to scratch
my head, in case they don't wave back,
and I stand on looking...intrigued
or askance: how else could you?

Good for Olivier

RONA ALTROWS

"WHAT PROJECTS ARE YOU WORKING ON THESE DAYS?"
an acquaintance asked.

"I'm helping Naomi compile a book on shyness," I said.

"What? You're not shy."

"Oh, but I am."

She looked at me, waited a beat. Laughed.

I felt hurt, but not surprised, as I had received a similar reaction many times throughout my life. But what is the face of
shyness? Does anyone know? I am the kind of shy that does not
necessarily show in the face.

To complicate matters, although the shy side dominates, I
also have a strong and well-developed not-shy side. Sometimes
nothing can stop me from approaching, talking to, laughing with
other people. I do plenty of readings, speaking engagements, and
so forth. All the more reason that, when my shyness begins to
take over, I am often not believed.

A shy/not-shy human is a frequently misunderstood one.

I can't predict when I'll move from shy to not-shy. The switch can
occur without warning, and when it does, I may find myself in a fix.

That's what happened some years ago, when I had a job with
a public relations side, involving occasional travel. On one trip, I
represented my company at a conference. I found the first two
days productive and enjoyable, as, in not-shy mode, I interacted
comfortably with people, handed out and collected business
cards and generally did my company proud. The others attending
the conference were either existing clients or prospective clients
of my company. On the third and final day, my company was
scheduled to host a five o'clock reception featuring the biggest
inducement at any gathering of adults in the so-called developed

world: an open bar. My bosses back home counted on high atten-
dance and budgeted a lot of money for that reception. As the face
of the company, I was expected to work the room thoroughly and
non-stop until the departure of the last guest.

At a little after four o'clock, I began to sense myself moving
into shy mode. Suddenly I felt apart, unto myself, disconnected
from anyone else. The idea of being around other people, of having
to perform socially, threw me into a state of terror. I was sure I
would not be able to do what was required of me.

So I retreated to my hotel room and sat still, willing myself to
transform back into not-shy mode in time for the reception. With
all my heart, I did not want to go.

I did go; it was my duty. But I could not pull out of shy mode
the whole time. It would probably have been better for my
company if I had stayed away and given the evening to reading.
I cowered in corners, made frequent and lengthy escapes to the
washroom, and talked to nobody, not even people I already knew.
I was so paralyzed with shyness I could barely raise my head. All
I could think of was flight, escape, the need to be alone. At that
reception my company had no human face.

That night I felt heavy, weighed down with awkwardness and
the knowledge of social and professional failure. Yet mere hours
earlier, I had experienced a sense of lightness, good humour, easy
fellowship with the many other people at the conference.

The flipping between not-shy and shy has been going on in
me as long as I can remember. Perhaps because I had a shy
father and a not-shy mother. Is there a genetic component to shy/
not-shy? Or do we find a place on the shy/not-shy spectrum
through socialization? I wonder if it even makes sense to characterize shy/not-shy as another of those heredity-versus-environment
mysteries. Maybe nature and nurture both contribute. Maybe
certain behaviours, reflecting either shy or not-shy, are reinforced
by our parents, while other behaviours reflecting the opposite are
squelched, so that we wind up at least appearing shy or not-shy
most of the time. Or maybe the origins of our ways of moving
through the world don't matter, and we should just concentrate
on self-acceptance.

When I was a little girl, school was the centre of my social life, such as it was, and my favourite place. I loved the structured academic day, the reassuring routines, the lessons themselves, the half-pint bottles of milk for sale at recess. School also gave me opportunities to display my not-shy capabilities. In grade four, we had Afternoon Classics, a learning program that consisted of the teacher's reading the class entire great books in twenty-minute segments at the end of each school day. Miss Pearson, a halting oral reader, struggled valiantly through a couple of chapters of Mark Twain, but realized from all the fidgeting in the classroom that she could not hold her audience. One day after school, she took me aside and asked if I would mind reading in her place during Afternoon Classics. (Oral Reading was a subject, so Miss Pearson knew how every student sounded.) I was in heaven. I've always been a passionate oral reader, and my classmates did listen intently. It brought me such delight, such a sense of belonging, to bring them pleasure. Their silence allowed me to make subtle adjustments in volume and pace as needed. We got through *Tom Sawyer*; *The Wind in the Willows*; *The Lion, the Witch and the Wardrobe*. Not-shy-I performed well, delivered great literature to my classmates, and helped a good teacher out in the process. Does it get better than that?

Yet when awards day arrived, and all I was required to do was walk to the front of the school gym to receive a certificate, shy-I shook in my seat, was barely able to get up when my name was called, and had to let jelly legs carry me to my destination. As the adult in charge handed me my prize, I struggled to get out a simple word of thanks.

For me, shyness has always been enmeshed with anxiety. In adolescence and early adulthood I did a lot of acting. I liked growing into my part, rehearsing, hanging out with other theatre types. Getting out in front of an audience, however, was a problem. Before each performance, I was overcome with bashfulness and apprehension, which manifested physically in a maddeningly itchy chest rash, abdominal pain, and, sometimes, shaky legs. My father wisely suggested I hold back a little, to save myself. I did not know how to hold back. A director tried to reassure me by pointing out that Olivier also suffered from crippling stage fright. That was an interesting piece of intelligence, but it did not help me.

Once I had the lead role in a play. Minutes before curtain time on opening night, I announced to the director that I would not be able to go on. "I'm so sorry," I said. "I can't. I just can't."

"Rona," she said, "I did not give you this part because you can't do it, but because you can."

And I did. But it was tough.

At a certain point I had to decide whether to pursue a professional acting career. I was tempted to try and follow the pro route. The work fascinated me and fulfilled me creatively; the theatre environment and the people it attracted made me happy; and I had received plenty of encouragement from directors and critics. Still, I had to ask myself this question: Am I willing to go through a lifetime of pre-performance introversion and visceral terror? In the end, I could not bear the idea of living in such reliably recurring fear. So I quit. True, Olivier stuck it out. Good for Olivier.

Here's one thing I have slowly come to understand, after years of trying to master or mask shyness: when I am in shy mode, so be it. I don't have to master, mask, or fight shy-me. I can allow myself to be one rather than splitting into two parts: shy-me and fighting-shy-me. It is liberating not to struggle to be something that, at shy moments, I simply am not.

So, if I find myself moving into shy mode at a social event, I may retreat from whatever group I happen to be part of, and instead converse one-to-one with someone I know well. Or I may offer to help the host by setting out food, washing dishes, retrieving a case of beer from the basement fridge. Doing a task helps me stay healthy when I'm shy. I may leave the scene for a few minutes for a walk around the block. I may simply thank my hosts for a lovely time and leave. I have options.

I think we tend to assume that not-shy is a preferable state to shy. Not for me, now that I accept my shy/not-shy nature. True, in not-shy mode I find it easier to make a necessary business call to someone I don't know well or have never met. In not-shy mode I navigate my way through life less laboriously. But in shy mode, I am more acutely aware of other people's feelings, more obser-vant, more attuned to my environment. There is much to be said for shy mode. In not-shy mode, it's party time. I miss a lot of what is going on around me in terms of other people's experience.

In recent years I have finally come to understand that shy mode deserves as much respect as not-shy mode, and I have restructured my life so that, for hours on end, I do not need to interact with more than one person. Then, when I am out and about, I can enjoy other people properly.

So far I've had no complaints from others. And more impor-tantly, I am at peace with myself.

MICHELINE MAYLOR

Insecurity

Oh, my little pedigree of reading in the can!
Slim and dim at dinner parties
heeled by the beautiful and interesting.

What can be done to glamour up
a witty quip in the starshine
of all these teeth?

How to be shy

KERRY RYAN

HOW TO BE SHY: THE HUG

Receive only, never initiate

Recognize the signs:
a trespasser entering your body's atmosphere,
arms gaping like a B-movie vampire

Hesitate,
be certain you are the target

Hesitate again,
ensure maximum awkwardness

Miscalculate the landing of limbs,
hastily rearrange
Realize your breasts are a thrust jumble,
that you're gripping a coil of fat
in a way that might imply judgement

Let panic escape through your face
as it perches on his or her shoulder

Be alert to variations:
palm corroding your back,
lips rasping the west side of your face

Allow a small sound,
that of a trapped animal, to escape
Pretend this hasn't happened

Count to one (silently), release

Hold the relief inside your lungs
until you've retreated a safe distance

Let everything you know
about this person drain like a sewer
hungry for thunderstorm

Open your mouth
Wait
Close your mouth

Stare at his or her chin
until a self-conscious hand
is lifted to hide it

If you are in Winnipeg,
pose an inane question
to which you know the answer:
snow

Repeat:
mosquitoes

Ask about pets or lovers,
then offer condolences

Wonder why you're suddenly
using hand gestures,
why you're laughing
Suspect that words may not be leaving
your mouth in the correct order

Hope so fervently
for the light to change,
line to move, movie to start
For a fire alarm, flash flood, heart attack,
that it shows
in the flushed clench of your face

If a foreign hand flashes open,
remove your damp palm from its pocket,
(dislodging shredded tissue)
allow it to be shaken

Forget the face even as you look at it
Let his or her name bounce
off your forehead

Speak your own too softly
Repeat it, step closer,
repeat it, step closer

Later, when you're called
by a name one degree from correct,
consider changing
your driver's licence

Stand next to the chips,
never move

Gaze thoughtfully
into the middle distance,
as if heartily amused
by the doorways and tunnels
of your own mind

Eavesdrop on conversations
roiling around you,
smile at the apropos comments
you choose to swallow whole

Practise invisibility

Drink your wine too fast
And the next glass

Select a book, skim the jacket,
nod knowingly
Work your way through each shelf,
ditto the CDs

Seize the first person
who speaks a word to you,
latch on like a long-lost friend, a twin
from whom you were separated at birth

SHAWNA LEMAY

Shybrightly

IN THE YEARS between high school and university, those years
in which I learned to breathe thinly and sharp, I somehow sum-
moned the courage to take an evening class. It doesn't matter
what the subject was, the ruins of Rome, a brief history of God,
the Etruscans, or the Unicorn in art and literature, it doesn't matter.
At the break, after student introductions and the terrifying intrica-
cies of the course outline, a woman from the class came up to
me in the lavatory, and said to me out of the ghastly greenish-
yellow haze of the mirror, there's help for people like you.

Not everyone believes shyness needs to be cured. In his autobiography, Gandhi devotes a chapter to shyness. For him, shyness
was an advantage, a boon. He says:

> Beyond occasionally exposing me to laughter, my constitutional
> shyness has been no disadvantage whatsoever....Its greater benefit has
> been that it has taught me the economy of words....a thoughtless
> word hardly ever escapes my tongue or pen....Proneness to exaggerate,
> to suppress or modify the truth, wittingly or unwittingly, is a natural
> weakness of man and silence is necessary in order to surmount it....My
> shyness has been in reality my shield and buckler. It has allowed me to
> grow. It has helped me in my discernment of truth.

Thoughtless words, words that have escaped my tongue, are a
plague to me, horrible blisters. The trouble being that when I am
called upon to speak, there is a darkness that envelops me, a cloud
that descends and takes me in its unappeasable woolly arms. But
I don't worry, since I know there is help for people for me.

In fact, I've never thought of seeking help. Shyness, I must have known all along, is my shield and buckler. Not everyone is so adorned.

Breathe consciously, is one bit of advice I came across recently when I looked up "shyness" on the web. Good advice, I think. Very good. The affliction of shyness, says one particular web site, causes one to "stop breathing, freeze, and attempt to become invisible when afraid." I had never thought that my lifelong preoccupation with learning to become invisible was an unwanted side-effect but, rather, the potential gift of shyness. If only I could become more shy, then perhaps, at last, I could learn to become invisible. I can say, however, from quite a bit of experience, that not breathing, at least not this alone, does not do the trick.

⋮ When I was in grade three, the doctor said that I had an S curve developing in my spine, and also that my lungs were undersized. He recommended exercise, swimming, and cycling. Apparently walking with the red wagon to the library, filling it with books, and walking back and settling into the orange fake leather chair that could be spun to face the corner of the room, my body a perfect and nearly invisible "S," was not sufficient. For my birthday that year in May, I was given a state-of-the-art bike, also orange, for some unknown reason, and it's only now that I notice this coincidental detail. That spring my parents decided to build a pool at the cabin. There would be no running water or plumbing in the house (we were learning to rough it, after all), but we would have a swimming pool. A friend with a Bobcat came and dug the hole, and then the rest was done by hand. I ignored the technical difficulties, the mixing and pouring of cement-like substances, the installation of skimmer and heater and whatnot. What I was transfixed by was the excavated pile of dirt and muck laden with rocks and other odd bits from eight feet below. I washed, sorted, and boxed. No one bothered me, which seemed to me remarkable. They looked at me, I thought then, as if I was spellbound, other. There were two worlds, one busy and full of laughter and intense discussion of myriad technicalities, and the other mine, slow and fine, silent, and strewn with new-discovered jewels. Two worlds, separated by a cellophane membrane, a curtain. Now, the mother of a five-and-a-half-year-old, I understand that one never interrupts a busy child with even so much as a smiling glance. The membrane is all too permeable.

All that summer, I breathed evenly through my runt lungs. I learned also how to swim that summer, never having managed anything other than a frantic dog paddle until then. My mom taught me the front crawl, the intermittent breathing, the perfect deep breaths in between strokes. But my favourite was swimming to the bottom and holding my breath there as long as possible, eyes closed, disappearing from the surface, unmoored and yet held, held in the glorious invisible freedom of the depths.

To swim, to become fluid, in this place that had been so recently solid earth, was an odd sensation. I'm not sure what to do with it, but I can almost conjure it for myself, this sensation. This breathless, held, dark knowing of the absence and the presence and the fluidity of the depths.

⋮ There is a kind of shyness into which fear and humiliation cannot enter. I know this first from the summers of my childhood where I slipped away into the forest, horses following. I would try to lose myself, in myself and in the forest. I went shyly through the trees, to the trees. For shyness, too, is a stance, a way of being—silent, seeing, reserved, a little off-kilter. Shyness is an approach, it might be said, just like any other approach.

⋮ "Speaking," says Fernando Pessoa, "is the easiest way of becoming unknown." One of the contradictions of shyness is that I want to be known and, at the same time, invisible. Speaking undoes me, it removes me from the mysterious core of being. Speaking, I am not myself, and therefore cannot be known. But then, it's true that we are not just one self. When I speak, I am my own stunt double, mouthing words that I imagine will be dubbed in properly by the real me in the editing stages.

When I began writing poetry, I came across the story of how the poet Gwendolyn MacEwen would at times become physically ill before a reading. By all accounts she was a mesmerizing reader, sultry and mysterious. For no good reason, I have always illogically connected MacEwen with Emily Dickinson. Archibald MacLeish says that "there is nothing more paradoxical in the whole history of poetry, to my way of thinking, than Emily Dickinson's commitment of the live voice to a private box full of pages and snippets tied together with little loops of thread." To me, it's sane behaviour. I have at all times reserved in my closet a box full of bits of thread and ribbon and twine.

In my undergraduate years, I was sure to take classes that wouldn't require any oral presentations. When one popped up on a syllabus, I dropped the class. For one required class, there was no backing out. The paper shook, I turned red. I'm sure it was a nerve-wracking sight to watch, and I'm filled with pity for those who had to endure it.

I almost fainted in the bathroom at the Café Soleil the night of my first poetry reading, which was with several other readers. I have a distinct memory of the wood grain of the rough floor-boards in that café. I remember that the doors to the loo required a great deal of jostling to open and close, and that I thought I might be trapped there when my name was called. But I did make good my escape, and I did read, and afterwards I went home and tied up the rumpled, sweated-upon pages with bits of twine.

Later, I joked with a friend about a performance poem that I developed, titled *Red*. If all else failed at a reading, this would most likely succeed.

Flash forward several years. I'm at the Old Vic on the University of Toronto campus, reading, along with three other poets, to a packed house, people standing up at the back. I'm the third reader. The only thing I remember about the first two—Sonnet L'Abbé and Lorna Goodison—is that they are impossibly good, dramatic, poised and confident. I'm breathing. Raggedly. Consciously ragged. Stunned by fear. My one thought, what a blessed life I've led; this is as afraid as I've ever been.

What does it mean to always be attending to breathing? What truth resides in these shallow breaths, the wild and tumultuous, and the gorgeous sweeping ones?

⋮ My name is called, I rise, I'm on the stage, this small book I wrote in my hand. I'm there with my shield and buckler. The light from the television camera is on my face, warm, golden, pale. I read, serene, calm. It's the stunt double, of course. But it's done. The next reader, George Murray, begins with an air guitar performance. I'm envious. But my stunt double only plays the typewriter.

Afterwards I try to remember. Did I breathe? I have no recollection. It was like being underwater, that is all.

⋮ Last summer I wrote a poem in which I quote Baudelaire. He says, "Anything that falls short of the sublime is reprehensible." I know this to be true. And I sorrow before the requisite temptation to believe otherwise. My poem goes on from there and ends with awe at all that falls short. I don't mind bringing up this poem, because since then it's been haphazardly folded, loosely bound, and it now languishes in a size nine-and-a-half shoebox. This is all quite romantic sounding, though it's really not meant to be.

There is the sense of the word *shy* that also holds the meaning *coming up short*. Just a little shy of the sublime here. Yet another sense of the word is one that is often applied to horses, or small birds. *To recoil, to shrink.* There is an excess of spirit, and this is what causes the animal to skitter or flit, its path diverging in a sudden and dramatic shift. When you're riding a horse that has shied, the natural reaction is to right the course, return to the prior, usually beaten, path. What happens when you let the horse have its head? What happens when you give free rein to this excess spirit?

Flamingos, I learn reading an entry from the seventeenth century, are extremely shy and therefore difficult to shoot.

One of the last citations in the OED for the word *shy*, under combinations, is Joyce's use of the word *shybrightly*.

⋮ The world is at odds with the shy person. The world shies from the shy, and maybe this is proper. Do we want to read the world as a text? Misinterpretation is part of every reading, and the shy person must take some joy in confounding the wordless, curtained message.

Not everyone undervalues or fails to recognize shyness, but commonly the shy are thought to be aloof, brooding, sullen, self-superior, stuck up, and, often, stupid beyond words. They are indeed quite difficult to shoot.

"To speak falsely, even with a false cadence, is to betray oneself," says Susan Griffin, in *The Eros of Everyday Life*. When I first read this several years ago, I made a difficult pact with myself—to not betray myself. But I have already broken the pact too many times to count. It's easier to keep the pact in the refuge of writing, in the refuge of ink and paper. I can best translate the skittish cadences of my breathing when I am silent.

How to keep the pact? How to live behind the clear drapery of days? Poetry is one way, though its fit with the world is uneasy, awkward, and at times skittish. There is no possibility of putting bread on the table with poetry, and so the poet needs to walk through the curtain. The pact will be tested. One is called upon to speak, the utterance comes up short, shy. One breathes into and draws from that space—that insane gap between what was meant or hoped for and what was. These uneven, sweet, swallowing breaths.

In a book called *Hermits*, Peter France talks about the practice of hiring ornamental hermits in the late eighteenth and early nineteenth centuries. In the gardens of the English gentry it became all the rage to house a hermit in the requisite grotto. France says that it was fashionable to be thought a man of sensibility, but that the belief was "there is no point in doing anything for yourself if you can pay somebody to do it for you," and so these sensible gentlemen "employed people to be melancholy on their behalf." It was more appropriate to hire your hermit by reading the advertisements than to take one out yourself, since a self-respecting hermit wouldn't be reading the newspaper in the first place. One such ad reads, "A young man, who wishes to retire from the world and live as an hermit in some convenient spot in England, is willing to engage with any nobleman or gentleman who may be desirous of having one."

The falseness in this enterprise is readily evident. The scene is comic and sad. But I'm interested in the tensions and transferences, in the falseness intermingled with the real desire to retire from the world. The ornamental hermit position usually came with meals brought down by servants from the house. When guests came, the hermit might be expected to sit at the entrance of the grotto gazing at a human skull, and let loose long, whickering sighs. What psychic pain would this cause the poor reclusive soul? This was the cost of retirement, to act the part of the hermit, to engage in these temporary lapses of one's true self. To shy away from the truth enfolded into one's being.

⋮ I don't know how to live in the world. It's the question on so many people's minds these days. I'd like, some days, to be a convenient hermit, paid to be melancholy and shy on someone else's behalf. Even if I did, at long last, find such a job in the want ads, I don't think my family would be too glad about the position, and then too, I never can remain melancholy for long. So, as much as I like the idea, it's not possible, or even really desirable, for me to retreat from, to shy away from, the world. The question then, is how to live shyly in the world, and fearlessly.

What is this desire to be known and yet not known, invisible and solid at once? What is accomplished by attending to the breathing patterns of the shy? Nothing, maybe. I don't know. "The wind is said to be shy" (and again this is the OED), "when it will barely allow a vessel to sail on her course." How to be the shy wind to the vessel of the self? How to live in the world? One of the infinite possible answers: shybrightly, shield and buckler in hand. Shyfearlessly.

Stage Fright

CASSY WELBURN

My face is an egg I take,
step onto the bare stage
and hold up
blind in the spotlight,
unable to stay intact
my first day of theatre class.

"Speak," he calls. "Move."

I carry my body like a tub of blood,
carefully, so as not to spill anything,
even my lines, onto the scene.
His orders—"Stage left" and "Stage right"—
slosh in my head, tremble my thighs,
drain from memory.

"Well," he yells, "what have you got to say for yourself?"

A squeal from my throat—"Lend a hand"—
cracks open my voice like the unscrewing of a jar.
It startles the student before me,
who drops her script.

"Will you lend a hand—to lift the dead?" I struggle,
the desperate shriek of Antigone growing inside me.
"Or will I go alone to heap earth on the brother we love?"

She backs away. "No, I cannot," she whispers.
"It's forbidden."

I am alone now under the great proscenium arch,
staring into the darkness.
My knees begin to move by themselves,
I do not recognize the head that is twisting,
or my lunge toward her.
"Go to Creon then," I spit out.
"He is your care and protector."

"No, sister." I hear her protest. See her hands raised,
but I cannot stop myself.
Words break from me in disbelief.

"When you speak with him so loudly of the law," I cry,
reeling stage front at the commander marching toward me,
"Remember, God hates utterly the bray of bragging tongues!"

As I Stand Up Here Reading, Fear Holds My Hånd

CAROL L. MACKAY

Everything is accent aigu, cédille, circonflexe, umlaut
This is an audience I can't pronounce.
And yet, I am in front with him.

He says I'm becoming less than less,
He points out my poems have been infiltrated by sunsets and fireflies.
He says the sun is a hankie, bleached and oyster-stitched,
something to dab the eyes with.
Fireflies are, well, fireflies.

He tells me they know I am Loki,
That I brought down Asgård because they cast my fate.
He says predestination must always be fought. I have to agree.

But I smell aquavit, and I know, that last reference was way out there.
Fear is a lush.
It will take 16 lines and six schnapps to write him out,
to loosen the s's.
Eventually he sways. "Ja, Ja, you can do it. It's ease-y, my friend."

JANIS BUTLER HOLM

Are You an Introvert? Take This Simple Quiz

1. Your private life is
   a. rich and rewarding.
   b. an absolute hoot—especially the time you had sex with so-and-so.
   c. no one else's business, thank you very much.

2. A party is
   a. an opportunity for networking and career advancement.
   b. an excuse for drinking and bad behaviour.
   c. the smell and weight of strangers breathing your air.

3. In a crowd, you
   a. look for people you know.
   b. pinch bottoms with impunity.
   c. struggle not to scream, run, implode as though you were a dying star.

4. Sports and other arena events are
   a. safe outlets for human aggression.
   b. excuses for drinking and bad behaviour.
   c. best viewed on the television screen, where pugnacity and violence are tiny and contained.

5. Your local pub
   a. is your home away from home.
   b. has barred you from the premises.
   c. repeatedly offers the anguished re-enactment of human tragedy, which you prefer to avoid.

6. Your boss thinks you are
   a. personable and outgoing.
   b. fun on business trips (wink, wink).
   c. sensitive and strange but reliable enough to do most of his work.

7. At the grocer's, you
   a. chat amiably with neighbours.
   b. cruise the aisles for sexual conquests.
   c. shop quickly and efficiently, pausing only to admire rainbow stacks of fruit quiet in its skin.

8. Your cell phone is
   a. ringing constantly because you have so many friends.
   b. equipped with funny, clamorous ring tones.
   c. reserved for safety uses on the road, where there are always too many cars, too sudden dangers.

9. Your best friend is
   a. planning your surprise birthday party.
   b. sleeping with your lover.
   c. in fact your lover, who, miracle of miracles, seems to need no one but you.

10. You and your lover
    a. are thinking of buying a flat together.
    b. have noisy, boisterous fights followed by noisy, boisterous sex.
    c. read a lot, share hopes and dreams, make very witty comments about others' boisterous ways.

11. On the topic of introversion, you write
    a. a brief personal essay on what distinguishes you from the crowd.
    b. nothing at all. Who gives a damn about introverts?
    c. a mildly amusing magazine quiz that doesn't expose your private life (which is no one else's business, thank you very much).

STUART IAN MCKAY

a more
blissful orbit

because my hostas

gift me with flowers
the day before my birthday.

because the begonia i
stake this morning has

shed its crimson on the
stones of my garden path.

because the idealised

seven apricots i buy
from the blonde woman
in the market. the perfect

fiction of a smile between us

Women
Friends

BRIAN CAMPBELL

Today all my women friends
visit me, one by one,
to lament on my shoulder.
"Men are such liars," they tell me.
"All they want is sex, sex, sex."
"...and would you believe
after all these months
he phones me back and says
he loves me, he wants to
win me again, of course
it's all such bullshit."

I, of course,
must admit, agree.
Men are lechers, I tell them
—and most, unscrupulous liars.
Ninety percent don't make love to their women:
they masturbate
inside them.
Maybe a hundred percent.
Women to these men
are tough planks or spreading trees
to be chopped and burned to feed
a white-hot, dying
flame,
an ocean repository
into which their milky rivers
of orgasm
must exhaust.

Of course
my women friends agree.
They say things like, "Exactly."
They are charmed
by my perceptivity.
But me—I'm different.

Honest, they tell me.
Sensitive.
Friendship, we agree, that's
the important thing.
Friendship.
And these lips that ache so much to kiss,
this body, to merely hold and be held,
this prick,
this hard, throbbing
prick
will simply
go on aching
indefinitely,
with these, my
women
friends—
because I'm different, they tell me.
Honest.
Sensitive.
Because I never lie with them.
Because I never lie with them.

Shy—10 Ways

RUSSELL WANGERSKY

HER CATS WON'T LEAVE THE DOORMAT, and I know they're afraid she isn't coming back.

I know because I'm afraid of exactly the same thing.

The hallway glows with the incandescent light on the yellow paint, and the cats lie on their stomachs, front paws outstretched, still like statues, except for the occasional flicking ear.

Tonight, supper is tomato and red-pepper soup poured straight from a carton into a pot. The carton boasts the soup is made with real cream. "Stir on low heat—don't allow to boil."

The box goes on to suggest serving the soup with "a grilled vegetable, pesto, and goat cheese sandwich," or else "a tuna salad wrap with lemon-dill mayonnaise, cucumbers, and sprouts." I imagine, stirring, that if I had either of those choices, I wouldn't really need the soup.

One: I always buy a twelve-inch ham sub, extra cheese, tomatoes, lettuce, no sauce—the same order every time. My office at the news-paper is in a mall, so I'm downstairs a couple of times a week, and the regular sandwich makers in the food court storefront all know me. They like to tell me my order before I can say it, and when there's someone new on the cash register, one of the regulars always says, "He gets the discount—he works in the mall." It's a buck or so off, and all you have to do is say you work there. "I work in the mall"—simple enough, right? But I never have. Not even once. I can read from my books to a couple of hundred strangers, stand up at the front of an auditorium and read the dangerous personal pieces, the sharp and wounding parts about my sex life, but I can't tell someone I legitimately deserve the discount.

November now, and the house is dark too early in the evening. The big window in the kitchen is like a drab, flat painting, lost without daytime's depth: orange sky from the streetlights, the matte black cutout shapes of the houses hulking out past the backyard. Bare black tree branches reach in from the edge of the frame. The leaves are all down from the maples, and I walk from room to room as if jumping from puddle to puddle in the yellow pools spilled from each individual light fixture. There is no one in any of the rooms, no one except for me, but I enter each one cautiously anyway, wary just in case.

Like travelling the sharp and sudden revelations of a train passing through a string of new subway stops, except I'm the entire wandering train, shuffling along there in my sock feet. White athletic socks, always.

It is a big house, bigger when you're alone, two storeys and a full basement down beneath, a house knuckled in close to a street that seems all the busier because cars come by so near to the front windows. The kind of place where you need curtains, even in the daytime, because the narrow strip of sidewalk is right on the other side of the glass. Lying on the couch, you can catch snatches of people's lives as they walk by, people talking openly and carelessly, sure no one could possibly hear them. Fugitive sentence fragments, harvested and saved as carefully as if they were beach-shells.

"If your mother says that one more time, I promise I'll..."

"I can't imagine why she thinks that's unreasonable, taking out..."

"You just don't listen."

Not paying attention at the crucial time, I let the soup boil.

The pot, left alone in the kitchen, has come to its own angry conclusion without any input from me.

Outside, wind cuts corners, and the leaves, yellow and brown, hiss and rattle across and down the sidewalk. They dance on their drying tips so they skitter like dried-up spiders or hard-shelled beached crabs. The cats don't like the sound, and they rush up anxious from the mat and onto the hillside of the sofa, nosing their way through the curtains to see what's making the noise, their tails big and alarmed. When they calm, they head back to their mat.

She brought the cats down here first by air, even before she moved, cat-carrier travel aided by veterinary drugs. One is small and ginger-coloured, the other larger, orange and white, and given to ceaseless meowing. Sometimes, the little one attacks the big one for no discernible reason, as if intent on solving some small frustration by lashing out indiscriminately.

At the Toronto airport, she says, she let them out of the cat carrier, and the big one's eyes were rolled right up in its head from the drugs, and it dragged its back legs around like it was paralyzed. Once they got here, the smaller one wedged itself tight behind the furnace and wouldn't shift, not even for tuna right out of the can. Then the larger one hunkered down behind the dryer, fixed in place big and round like the Cheshire Cat, but nowhere near as jolly.

There's laundry in that dryer right now, our laundry all tangling together, and I can hear the snaps and buttons sliding and clanking off the enamel.

Two: There is a short row of new shirts in my closet—some have been there for months. I'm still deciding if I can wear them. Any of them. Red—it might be a good colour. It might be a good colour on me. But is it too different? If I actually wear it, will the change be too abrupt? Will I jump out, will someone at work say, "Hey, is that a new shirt?" There are, in there, shirts that I will never wear—yet, paradoxically, love far too much to ever give away in the regular closet-cleansings. There are some that I love simply because I wish I was able to wear them.

The dryer has a faraway, incomplete sound, like neighbours arguing small arguments on their deck, the sort of sound that's supposed to speak of hearth and house pride the same way the smell of bread does. In this big empty house, it only sounds lonely.

"If I ever leave, the cats stay," she says. "I'm not putting them through all that again. I'm just not."

And I imagine costly therapy for abandoned step-cats, imagine the solitary click of their untrimmed claws on the hardwood, each meow a sound either bitter or lost, a serious white-coated doctor following their every meander with a notepad and urgently scratching pen.

I know I can't force things to stay the way I want, and that big changes appear suddenly from little things, like the jump of a serious earthquake from a pattern of tiny tectonic shifts. I know I can form words in my head, words that I can't ever force out of my mouth—and that, even if I do, they will be incomplete.

Three: Shy is strange. A spectrum of difficulties that, more than thirty years in, you just learn to moderate. It's far, far worse for some people than it is with me. There are people who can't speak to a stranger, who can't squeeze even a word out. I can talk, no problem at all, but only until it's about something I want. I can talk about you—I love to talk about you. I have a harder time getting beyond the shiny, easy public surface of me. The edges of your own particular shyness are clearly delineated. I know that. There are no smudged chalk borders, no lines that move easily or get pushed back, even with practice. Live inside shyness and you'll realize it's regimented as the precise and regular turning of gears in a clock. You can see things coming right toward you, tick-tock, each deliberate step at a time— you know the things you can do, and, after enough time, you learn the things you can't.

I could give any one of a countless number of reasons why I feel this way—why I fear this way. I've tried them all on, like clothes put on and then taken off again, without ever getting past the sliding mirrors in our bedroom.

But I'm getting ahead of myself.

⋮ Driving alone on a Sunday afternoon road far from anything, caught out on the Avalon barrens in heavy fog, there's a chapter-ending finality about every single kilometre.

I'm driving toward a town I've never seen, that hunkers down on the very foot of the Avalon Peninsula, a town pushed so far out into the ocean that it spends much of its time living under the grey weight of fogbanks. That is its constant, spring, summer, and fall, while winter brings the respite—if you can call it that—of regular, constant light snow.

The fog unfolds page by page—revealing a pond here, and a long, falling sideways heather-clad hill next—and I feel that abso- lutely anything is possible with the next turn, that any kind of monster could live right exactly there, that it could step out at any minute with a reach broad enough to put claws into both sides of the vehicle at once.

My hands hold the steering wheel too tight, and I can feel my muscles fighting the hard nubbled plastic. The car hugs the curves, and sometimes it's as if the car is on autopilot, my head going one way while my hands and the road interact all by themselves.

Things keep snapping into view in front of the windshield, like flash cards that haven't yet gotten around to revealing the order that underwrites their central pattern and explanation. Once, a white headstone, rough pockmarked old limestone, "CAREEN" all in yelling capitals across the front, so that it's hard to know for a moment whether it's a name or a shouted instruction. Another time, a small, lonely juniper tree, its branches crooked and bent and black with the condensing fog, and an angrier-looking tree I don't think I have ever seen.

Somewhere up ahead of me is Point Lance, a town whose name sounds like the tip of a needle seeking a boil, and I've driven by the side road that heads down to that town a hundred times, and never taken the time to actually make the turn.

But I turn down the road all at once anyway, despite the stories I've heard of a rough crowd down there, of former fox farms with wire fencing and sentry towers like miniature prison camps. Fox farms that smelled alternately of fox piss and risky investment, and, finally, the whiff of broken dreams.

The pavement is cracked and wrinkled all along the edges of the road, with the cracks all leading inwards, cracked like nature's just too damned tired of being kept at bay and has decided to slowly edge its way toward the yellow centre line—and I think that when the cracks reach that defining line, all man-made things will be necessarily finished here.

Behind me, the past is closing as fast as new things appear, history erasing itself with grey gauze: one moment, it's a shopping bag caught flapping in the endless wind, caught on the tip of one hedged branch and whipping against itself, and the next, the bag is gone as easily as if it had never been, and the present is an instant of a small stream threading its way into an overlarge corrugated culvert.

When I get to Point Lance, it is not what I'd expected.

Not because I didn't expect small and hardscrabble and tough, not because I didn't expect wood smoke and flat empty windows as unyielding as mirrors and an empty twisting road with not one single living person in sight, but because I didn't expect the beach.

A beach like that—I think I would have heard about that, at least from someone careless enough to let it slip, the "Oh, you want to see a hidden gem" kind of thing.

The sand is long and red and ruled flat by the tide, so that the only thing left is the tracks from a large dog, running away, running fast so the claws dig in far deeper than the pads, and there's no way at all of telling just when it was last here. No telling whether it's still here, just out of sight up ahead in the fog, waiting. And the wind is blowing hard, driving the fog against my skin, and I can feel it in my hair. I hate my feeling my hair move.

Four: Forty-nine years old, and I still can't stand it when someone points out I've just gotten a haircut. My mother used to cut my hair in grade school, always the same way. Straight across the front, that cut everyone in my class called a "bowl cut," as if I'd had a mixing bowl over my head while Mom worked the scissors across my fore-head in a straight line. Then the clippers up the back and right over the mess of cowlick that would never lie down. She had no concep-tion why the abrupt change—from longer hair to no hair—would bother me. Yet I know she was crushed the very first time I told her I wanted someone else to cut it. The hairdresser who cuts my hair now has been cutting it for twenty-five years. If she's not available when I call, I get my hair cut on another day when she is.

Coming down the road, I have passed several houses with big chain-link enclosures housing very big dogs, the kind of dogs that tear at the fences with their front paws even though they know it's fruitless to try and break through—maybe just so they can see their actions' effect on me as I drive past. I have seen no trees or fire hydrants or other strangers, nothing else in this town to serve as canine distraction.

The first thing I think is that if there is still a dog loose out there, it's going to be a big dog, and it will be delighted, in its private, revenge-filled way, to meet with me. It's foolish, I guess, to believe angry dogs are always in a rush to settle someone else's scores on your flesh.

At least I know where the dog isn't, where it can't be.

I know it isn't at the end of the beach behind me, where the rocks come down from the cliff and jangle out into the water in jagged tumble. There, the sand is still unmarked, face unlined and in repose.

In the other direction, with the distant beach lost under the fog, it's not so easy to tell. My instincts warn me that there could be something out there. And you've always got to pay attention to the things your instincts are busy warning you about, even when you don't want to believe them.

The tide line is littered with the occasional shred of wrack and seaweed, and, strangely, a potato, and then another, right at the edge of the water, as if they'd been washed in, waiting for someone to save them. Amazing how a mind can wander, how just for one shimmering moment I picture a huge passenger-steamer, taking on water fast, all of its potatoes abandoning ship into the cold North Atlantic, a colossal and tragic tuber epic, tears running from oh so many potato eyes.

I kick a few potatoes along the sand, looking over my shoulder guiltily once or twice to be sure no one is looking.

Five: For five excruciating years, I worked in television as a news reporter. Seems an impossible job for someone who's shy. Perhaps— but when you're desperate, you invent solutions. Coping mechanisms. Stopgaps that can make impossible things work, because there are mortgages and credit cards and bills that have to be paid. I learned to watch my stories only on the monitors in the editing suites at the television station, never on an actual television at home. Pretended they were a private production, seen only by my cameraman, my editor, and me. Startled when anyone came up to me and talked about a news story I'd done: I was so completely deluded, I'd wonder where and how they possibly could have seen it.

·The beach at Point Lance stretches out red and even ahead, and stretches out sideways as well to the edge of the fog—the beach disappears before the waves even have a chance to break, although I can hear them out there, thundering in loud, then falling away all at once like their lips and teeth have been forced to bite into cotton wool at the very last moment.

I walk for a few more minutes until the wet heft of the wind settles in under my jacket, in around my neck where the skin is too soft, and then I head back for the car, where the gear shift and the pedals are all in the right place, and my hands feel right on the wheel again.

But what does this have to do with her?

Well, I guess the fact is it's all about her, from soup to sand.

Because I drive away from Point Lance with the idea that I just want to show her this place, that I want to give it to her—word-lessly, because that's sometimes all I am capable of—as simply as if I had done it up in wrapping paper and handed it to her, with the hapless idea that she will be as grateful to receive it as I will be happy to give.

Driving out of the small town, little more than a gaggle of houses edged in tight along both sides of the road—the passenger seat beside me empty—I come to a big new-looking bridge over a slow-moving, peat-brown river, and off to the right, a small old gravel quarry where they've dug up the stone for the road.

From the quarry, a small trail heads out east under the low cloud toward the shore, and there's just enough visibility to see a beach there as well, easily a couple of kilometres out of town, and I find myself wondering if the red sand as fine as flour runs out as far as that.

Because if it does, I think, we could park the car and head down there with a blanket, and we could both lie naked on the beach, far enough from everything that we could listen for the high whining bumblebee-thrum of the all-terrain vehicles coming and get back into our clothes, shaking the loose sand out of our sleeves and cuffs long before they had a chance to get there. You'd see them coming for miles, heads and handlebars hovering above the marbled oily ripple of the heat-shimmer, until they get close enough for their wheels to coalesce into tires, hubs and finally the long run of tracks, heading back and away.

I can imagine the flat smooth sand and her entire body there, stretched out long and smooth under the sun like hills and heather.

Because I know every single inch of her like Braille, and she's never minded Braille-reading before. I can imagine it, right down to the way the fine, dusty sand will catch and stick in those small starred patterns where the first skim of perspiration makes its careful way out through skin. Right down to the way that goose-bumps rise up and breath catches from the touch of fingers electric.

Six: For years, directing my lover with my hands, because I was too shy to put anything I wanted into words. Then, if something goes wrong, you can always claim that you were misunderstood. Not at all like words. I've always been too afraid to hear the clear danger of her spoken words in response.

I want to believe that, if we went there on that singular day, the sun would shine in a way I've heard it almost never does in Point Lance. The way it almost never does because the land sticks permanently out into the cold water and snags the ocean air like a fishing hook caught deep into the weave of some particularly stubborn and unyielding cloth. It is the way it is, like I am the way I am. Pouring words out here, but struck dumb when it is urgently important that I speak.

Seven: I even write shy. I write for people who don't know me. But for those who do, I hide other things in the words and sentences they might recognize. And for those who know me really well, there's often even more. It's not a parlour trick, not a game—it's not even really deliberate, at least not as a deliberate structure. I'm not trying to be deep—I'm trying to communicate. A column, an editorial, a short story: there are keys in all of them that are meant to unlock the particular, and I have particular people in mind when I place them. Semaphore, message in a bottle, Morse code—they say an experienced operator recognizes the touch of a familiar hand on the Morse key.

The soup is cooking with fat angry plops now, past tempered boiling, steam lurching up through the reddish liquid like fumaroles that snap open and closed on the edge of an impending stovetop eruption.

Perhaps my curse will always be not paying nearly enough attention at that crucial moment when everything matters. Perhaps my curse is that I know I won't be able to call for help when it does.

Not only has the soup boiled, it has burned as well, annealing itself into a hard skin on the bottom of the pot, and few kinds of sandwich would be able to save that. It has made a pattern exactly the same shape as the burner right there on the inside bottom of the pot, a pattern that screams out about the callous absence of careful stirring. A pattern that says "how could you?" with a hanging and unfinished ending, as though said by a stranger passing our street-front window and then disappearing, unseen, into the night.

Outside, the wind has gotten hard and blunt, rattling the screen door like it wants to come inside and can't understand the latch mechanism, and she'll be hard and blunt too—even her lips will be cold, I think, and a tremble shoots down somewhere through the long tendons in the backs of my thighs. By the time she gets here, walking fast, her head will be whirling with a thousand shards of ideas like broken glass in a hurricane. I'll have to wait to see which way she wants to turn, whether she'll head upstairs with her lips seamed shut or whether she'll want to fall together on the floor. Or maybe, as I always fear possible, she won't be home at all, swept away on the white-breaking crest of something or someone too amazing to resist.

Bittersweet and frightening, exhilarating every time: I wonder if I'm always going to get to dream this way, whether I get to have a whole life looking at changing mental sketches of tomorrow, or if one day, it will just run out of me like air out of a flattening tire. If it will become too much effort or too little reward, too much fear and too little wonder.

Eight: I am full, stuffed full with things I feel justified thinking, but that I can't find a way to say. The words tumble and crash over each other, hundreds of them—but I remain mute, even when an argument rages all around me.

Right now, I can draw a thousand ways that any single thing might happen, a million different ways in which next week or next month could unfold. My hands are always full.

The only thing that's hard to conceive is that we could end up alone and clinging together, each depending by necessity on the other, our individual worlds toppled into one by the absence of anything else. Because there is too much else.

The thing is, in just a year or two she's found her way into this town like a splinter into soft flesh, found her way in far better than I've been able to in two decades. And she doesn't need me, not socially. She sits in her own brilliantly lit circle, overhung and surrounded by her own chandelier of main and subsidiary cut crystals.

Nine: I stay close to walls. "Mixers" are excruciating. Many of my clothes are deliberately dark or plain. I don't want to look like I care about how I look, and I don't want to look like I don't care. I just don't want anyone to look. I want to leave anywhere without fanfare or goodbyes, slipping outside and away even when doing exactly that is plainly rude. I can talk to anyone, as soon as I see them well enough to think of them as someone. I watch all the time, especially the people who move so easily out there in the world. How amazing, how free it would be to have none of that baggage. I've met the un-shy, and I know they have no idea of the simple gift they've been given.

She has friends now whose names I've never even heard before, a circle of friends that gets larger and larger like a brush fire getting bigger with every single step outwards—it's gotten to the point where it's creating its own wind, that the whole thing is close on to unstoppable, that the fireground officers should be calling the waterbombers in with more than a little edge of panic in their voices. She tells me the things her friends say and do, even though the names seem as distant from me as if she were chanting constellations in order of diminishing familiarity: "Cassiopeia, Andromeda, Taurus, Octans, Pavo, Grus."

She charms them.

She can catch them with something as simple as her eyes. I know it well, the way those eyes can be so big and alert and attentive. Or else she snags them with something like the lasso of the U-Haul story, setting the rope gently around them and drawing them back in with the steady pull, so even that they can't even feel the tug.

The U-Haul story. The U-Haul story is hers, and I won't touch it.

It's enough to say that she drove hundreds of miles to get here, practically single-handed, a drive filled with rising, cresting catastrophes amping up with every passing mile, but she can fill in those blanks. And she'll tell you that if anyone is a poster-child for commitment and dedication and a willingness to throw it all in to make a clear and definite choice, she's the one. And the U-Haul story is her absolute, unquestionable, permanent proof.

But like I said, that's her story.

She knows the cadence better than I do. She's from out west, and knows about catching things with thrown ropes. Me, I'm from the east, all my lines have hooks on the end instead, and hooks leave marks that heal into small white permanent scars.

Ten: I depend on the idea there are people who hear the message I send, however carefully and lightly it is telegraphed. I can read out loud easily when I find that one sympathetic set of eyes in the audience: I can write about anything if I can imagine being read by just one single person. It's hard for me to grip the idea that a book could be in any living room, that something I've put down could be open to the critical examination of someone I've never met. My newspaper's circulation is in the thousands: I write each column for a single person, and not the same single person either.

She's probably telling the U-Haul story right now, each note and pause and step in perfect place and pitch, and enthralled is not at all too strong a word to describe the rapt faces of her listeners. I know I should be glad of that, glad that she's found a place here all her own; I should be glad, not jealous—or worse, afraid.

I've poured the burned soup into the bowl anyway.

Perhaps she and I will get to see the beach above Point Lance on the one single day when the sun comes out. Maybe we will lie in the sun and on the sand mere microns apart, a million miles from either November or the chilly winds of doubt.

I know—I know—that it's all there in my hands, that it's in my words, if I can only force them out. But I also know that force would require an absolutely unconventional bravery.

She says she'll always be back, says it thrown out behind her like she is reaching out one smooth hand, ruffling hair or fur before she goes. The cats don't believe her, either. And I hold shy in my hands ten ways, always.

STEVEN HEIGHTON

Drunk
Judgement

A night address

The world is wasted on you. Show us one clear time
beyond childhood (or the bottle) you spent your *whole*
self—hoarding no blood-bank back-up, some future aim
to fuel—or let yourself look foolish in reckless style
on barstool, backstreet or dancefloor, without a dim
image of your hamming hobbling you the whole while.
Voyeur to your own couplings, you never did come
with them, did you, even when you did? You said Hell
is details, when Hell was just the cave, the concave-
mirrored skull you dwelt inside, your left hand
polishing while the other shook to clinch a deal—
Provide, provide! Sure, in the end, like any soul
you were endless *and yets*—brave, deft with phrases, kind—
three cheers for you. Too closed to want what others love
you vetoed life—

        were there other worlds to crave?

When Love Was Grey & Timid

I.B. ISKOV

In the pale glow of sky light
yesterday's stones crumbled
under reserved feet.

I never wrote poetry—
I was lean and did not know
how to find nourishment.
The atmosphere was a pastel continual smile.

Something was missing.
There was no shadow on the shine;
there was nothing but stone and air
together like conspirators
breaking space.

I was a naive virgin
in white collar and black patent.

While beauty degenerated,
contrary colours
painted my fabled utopia.

I admit I embraced inhibited love
at Bathurst and Finch
at a late hour
in the company of trucks
blurring my vision
like a surrealist tragedy.

SHIRLEY LIMBERT

Redder Than a Canadian Sunset

DID BEING A LESBIAN CAUSE MY SHYNESS, or did shyness push me into being a lesbian?

According to recent studies, the latter could not be the case, so that leaves me with lesbianism as a reason for shyness. We will see.

At age five, with my best friend Mary in tow, I headed to our local church across the road from my childhood home in London, England, and asked the ever-present verger whom we should ask to marry us. You know what happened next. He spoke to our mothers, and we were not allowed to play together again. I was not shy then, although I might have already been a lesbian.

So when did this long-term debilitating shyness overtake me?

As a very small child, I was regularly asked to sing or recite in front of family and friends. "Come on, Shirley, show Auntie Winnie how nicely you can recite 'There Are Fairies at the Bottom of My Garden' (or sing 'Danny Boy' or dance 'The Sailor's Hornpipe')." The awful feeling began in the region of my belly button, making my stomach clench, and moved up my body like a volcano until, in seconds, eruption time arrived, and my face became hot, sweaty and bright red, luminescent in fact, if I'd only had the word then. I longed for oblivion. All I could think of at that point was the wave after wave of heat spreading across my cheeks, neck, and for all I knew everywhere else on my little pulsating body, there for the entire world to see. I tried to run, but some family member or adult friend of my parents caught me, and my quavery little voice cried," No, no," and I dissolved into tears and hung my head, only to be sent to my room in disgrace.

Why did my parents and teachers torture me in this way, you ask? They all told me I was shy and I needed to be "brought out" of myself. I was asking for attention, they said, and I was to just do as I was asked without any fuss, and all would be well. I could not bring myself to do as they asked. My shyness was my fault they said; I should try to please. As if I didn't want to, as if I wouldn't have given anything to smile and prance about as they asked.

The feeling of impending doom wasn't necessarily caused by something I had done or not done. Anything could set it off, and then my flushing face made me, I felt, the centre of attention. I would stand glowing, shining, and glistening while onlookers, classmates, and teachers alike unhelpfully pointed out my disability. For that's what it is. A disability!

At school, if someone farted and filled the classroom with noxious gas, I would be the one sitting at my desk, glowing. In dance class, if someone was out of step, I would be the one looking at my feet, wishing the floor would open and take me in; I hid my pulsating face though I never made a mistake in dance. Why did I always feel culpable? Others made mistakes and I suffered remorse, and in some cases I was punished. Singled out because I was the blushing party, therefore I must be the guilty one. Or so it seemed to me.

Once I was old enough to understand that not all people suffered in the same way as I, then shyness and the subsequent and ever-present ability to flush, blush, or flash became more difficult to bear. The two were, in my mind, inseparable; walking to school was fraught with fear of seeing someone I knew and being spoken to, or, worse still, meeting girls from my school who, I was convinced, were laughing at me for being naive, for not wanting to talk about clothes with them or to giggle about boys. I had no idea what to add to their conversations about any of these things. I was not interested. I was terrified of being singled out in class to read or answer or perform a task. Although I was one of the brightest students, I endeavoured to make myself appear one of the least brainy. At exams I was fine alone in my world. I could shine. Just don't look at me!

Consequently, I aced my way through grade-school exams and started on my life's journey. Secretly, oh so deep in my heart, I wanted to write, and I did so. I put pen to paper, no PCs then, and created a mask for myself. Something I could hide behind. I produced reams of childish writing that as therapy might really have helped; but without someone to translate it, I was back where I started. In fact, having no one to bounce my thoughts off, I became more and more isolated. Soon my parents were at their wits' end.

By age thirteen, I was well on the way to becoming monosyllabic in front of other people.

Although I joined a dancing class at my mother's command, for she was frantic about my shyness by now, and therapy was not an option for a middle-class child of the late forties, I continued to hide my light under as many bushels as I could find.

But back to my first conjecture. Did being a lesbian cause my shyness or result from it?

My five-year-old self had already picked up the idea that, as a female, I would be in the wrong to fall in love with another female.

What happened? Celia happened. Celia who lived next door.

We did not go to the same grade school, so had little contact with each other until Grammar School. One day in our first term, as we both ran for the bus, I felt a quick tug at my heartstrings. We arrived at the bus at the same moment, and Celia stepped back to let me on. Her dark hair stood on end in the breeze, and her brown eyes smiled at me. I smiled back, mumbled something unintelligible as thanks, and boarded the bus. She followed. Celia sat next to me, Celia talked to me. I did not react with diffidence or timidity; I fell in love.

Celia and I became best friends, and Celia and I eventually explored first tentative kisses and gentle gropings beneath our school tunics. We became inseparable; my mother breathed a sigh of relief: I had a best friend like everyone else, therefore I must be normal, whatever she thought "normal" was, and she stopped pushing me to do things. I became less stressed and was even known to stand in class and respond to a question without blushing. I answered when spoken to at home, and tried hard to understand the jokes my school friends made.

However, the inevitable happened when we were fourteen. One teacher reported us for being "too friendly" and not having other companions. Apparently, she thought we should spend more time with other girls, giggling in the locker room or sitting in the cafeteria, gossiping. She spoke to the principal, who spoke with our mothers. Long story short, we were separated in class-rooms and during recesses, and Celia's mother picked her up after school and drove her home. We were not allowed to see each other at all. What we were doing was disgusting and unnat-ural, according to the principal, and I was dragged off to the local priest to confess. After a year and a half of feeling it was not entirely my fault, I was back to isolation and guilt over everything. I talked to the priest, told him I did not think I'd done anything wrong, so of course I could not repent, and I wasn't prepared to say I wouldn't do it again. After all, I had found a measure of comfort and happiness with Celia, and we had loved and trusted each other.

Through my school's dancing class, I was lucky enough to receive a scholarship to stage school, and about the same time, Celia's family moved. I was miserable. My mother took me to see the priest once more.

"But my child, if you are not remorseful for those actions, you cannot receive absolution. You will continue to live in a sinful state. May God bless your soul." There was also a lot of talk about hell and excommunication, and I left no longer a member of my church. I was fifteen.

Dancing was my only joy. I excelled, put on makeup, went on stage in front of audiences, and toured with a dance company. My life, although not easy (I still blushed at every mention of my name) was bearable, and when on stage I became another person, self-assured and full of stage presence. Putting on makeup gave me permission to be the person I wanted, besides which, it hid my blushing. I mixed well with the other girls in the corps de ballet, and they ignored my shyness, in fact helped me over difficult times. I did well at covering my timidity by not engaging too much with others.

Then along came Selena. I realized at first glance that here was another lesbian, and later she told me it was first glance for her, too. We got to know each other, I was elected to help teach her our dance routines, and sure enough she came out to me. I, of course, blushed redder than ever before at the word "lesbian," although I knew myself one. I told her about my life with Celia, and she smiled and hugged me.

I can honestly say that in the years Selena and I were together, I could count the number of times shyness overcame me, on the fingers of our four hands. Why? I think it was a mixture of being accepted by someone I really cared about and feeling she had my back at all times. I came home to her, told her anything, and although it was sometimes difficult, I knew eventually it would be okay. I trusted her and knew she trusted me. Our break-up was a year-long process, and we did all we could to make it easier on each other. Afterwards, she became involved with someone else and moved to Australia. She loved and loves me still, and I feel I owe her, at least in part, for my break with debilitating shyness.

Not that I got over it in one fell swoop. I didn't. Even now, years later and an ocean away, if I catch myself thinking of an embarrassing moment, and I know we all have them, I blush redder than a Canadian sunset. Even when I am alone. I have to force myself sometimes to go to gatherings or parties, or to speak in public, but I do those things as often as possible, and with each victory comes a soupçon of confidence. Some residual guilt of uncertain origin still hangs around somewhere, but I can handle it much better now.

Did being a lesbian cause my shyness? Of course not, but as a lesbian, acting on my feelings, living the life I was meant to live, and being loved—those things certainly helped me overcome the disability.

Fifty-some years later, I don't have so much invested in having the world love me as I did when I was younger. I've been lucky that those I love, love me. I am a retired social worker, in a relationship of nearly twenty years. Menopause gave me permission to flash, flush, and blush as much as I needed without having to explain or feel guilty; as estrogen waned, so did guilt and, believe it or not, shyness. I am comfortable in my skin, now.

MIKE DUGGAN

Laundry
Duty

In my first real job, the controller,
a tactile woman with an absent ring,
had me swinging from the hinge
of my shoulders

like a cat flap; a soft touch, one push
and she was through, there to peruse
my inner décor, which she instinctively knew
(like a precocious

child's spoken English)
was a little too pure to be taken
seriously. A few brief explorations
and she was connecting my *singleness*

with a clever rhyme for G&T, her *charity*
when buying the after-work drinks;
as I took my pint a knowing nod and wink,
"you look a little young to me."

Then, "telling me off" for being hungover next day,
my gullibility fuelled her laughter.
I felt like the innocent maid and she the master
and my heart took up the role, played

along whenever she held my eye:
drawing freshly laundered
blood from the liver (fully loaded)
and hanging it in my face to dry.

to the
red-haired girl
on eighth

WEYMAN CHAN

any nerve
splays its
background noise

my spy
aerially defers
the astroglider's last argument

eight feelers hunkered down on my sternum she
spins ownership over politicos
tight skinned in my opera

I have nothing
ancient or
medicinal to offer

sprockets blur
the floating road spray self
assembles its protein swing

why do I appear to
be happening
just as I stop and think about it

where if not here will her armour protect my concupiscence?
could I swing on handsprings
white flags

Riopelled over blinks and blunders that
got me behind
to get me here

little eye
save my stiff
puppet fluids

for climbing
if only your art
could crush me between the word and the thing

Common Loon

JEFF MILLER

ONE WINTER I haunted the library of a small city in Saitama Prefecture. The Penguin Classics sat on a shelf near the back, their titles written in white letters down black spines. In this corner of the world, the English canon was stripped to four dozen books, and by the end of my stay I had left only the thickest Victorian novels unread.

The librarian always recognized me; even this close to Tokyo a six-foot-tall white man with bleached blonde hair was an uncommon sight. She smiled and spoke to me in a soft voice while checking out my books on my ex-girlfriend's library card. I nodded and returned her smile, but didn't understand a word she said.

I read at the quiet chain restaurant next door. Its booths were narrower than the ones in the twenty-four-hour restaurant in the Canadian suburb where I grew up, but they were upholstered in a similar earth tone print. I refilled my coffee mug at the mechanized *durinku bar* several times over the course of the afternoon. Occasionally I called over one of the waitresses with a polite "Sumimasen," and pointed at a colour photograph of a grilled cheese sandwich on the otherwise illegible menu.

I bought a bicycle at a junk shop for eight thousand yen. It was grey, heavy, and identical to hundreds of others parked around town. Some days, instead of going to the library, I biked through mazelike streets lined with small houses until I reached the factories by the highway. One day I biked past a middle school marching band in bright red uniforms playing to an audience of senior citizens and mothers with strollers in the town square. I pulled over and watched them, recognizing one song as an arrangement of a J-pop smash hit that seemed to be playing on the stereo of every convenience store I walked into.

But whether I tried to distract myself with library books or bike rides to the edge of town, my thoughts would eventually return to my own stupid predicament. I had travelled ten thousand kilometres to a foreign country to be with a girlfriend who dumped me the night I arrived.

This was my real life: I was alone, adrift, and a fool. Sometimes, to delay going home in the evenings, I rode to a nearby bridge crossing a river whose name I didn't know. At the middle of its span the bridge widened to support a large sculpture of twisting glass columns. Beside it was a bench where I sat in the dark moping, smelling buckwheat and burnt tires on the night breeze.

Every night, no matter how long I managed to stay away, I eventually returned to the four-room apartment that the local school board had provided for my ex. It was nice enough, but everything that happened there was tinged with a kind of absurd misery and dark humour usually reserved for European art films. We talked and ate dinners consisting of fried vegetables covered in apple curry, a disgustingly sweet instant gravy that seemed a staple of inexpensive Japanese home cooking, and was regularly advertised on television. We watched Hollywood movies rented from the video store a few blocks away, and sometimes made out awkwardly in the narrow bed we were forced to share.

This life was a shadow of the plans we'd hatched in Ottawa before her departure. We had decided then that if I saved up for six months and got a work visa, our life together could be seamlessly transported from the orderly streets and redbrick houses of Ottawa to this industrial suburb of Tokyo. Bad idea.

I cried through that first night when she broke up with me, and the next morning my tears fell onto the thin pancakes served in the fourth-floor restaurant of the nearby department store. They were saturated with corn syrup, not Canadian maple syrup, several small bottles of which I had packed as gifts for any Japanese person who might befriend me or do me a kindness. It was December, and Christmas carols rang over the store's public address system even though Christmas is not a holiday in Japan. A garland of plastic pine boughs was strung along the walls of the cafeteria. I couldn't help thinking it resembled the restaurant in the Zellers on Merivale Road, near where I grew up.

"Kurisumasu kyaroru," my now ex-girlfriend said, trying to distract me. "That's what Christmas carols are called here. It sounds like English, but not."

"Kurisumasu kyaroru," she repeated.

⋮ I met Masako at a Christmas party in the small apartment of an English teacher. There were a handful of Anglophones teaching English in town—some Aussies, an Englishwoman, and a former alternative rocker from San Francisco. None were particularly interested in making friends with other foreigners. Everyone seemed to be counting down the days until their departure. I tried to look both nonchalant and engaged while avoiding actually talking to anyone at the party.

I was leaning against a counter in the crowded kitchen, nodding in the direction of an Australian guy telling jokes to a few young Japanese women, when Masako appeared beside me. She shook my hand and made an effort not to bow to a foreigner, but ultimately surrendered to habit. She was slim, and her tidy black bob swayed as she nodded. My ex had already told me of Masako's kindness. With the aid of her small electronic translator and rudimentary conversational English, this middle-aged housewife had taken it upon herself to guide the town's English teachers through banks, hospitals, municipal offices, and other houses of bureaucracy.

I had my answers ready. I had to reply to three questions before a Japanese person could be sure that my experience of their country was authentic: Do you like Japan? Can you eat with chopsticks? Have you tried Natto? Three yesses. My affirmative to the last question, about a fermented soy paste wrapped in nori that tasted like regurgitated cabbage, always got a laugh, the universal snicker arising from a visitor eating the local delicacy.

Where are you from? What is it like? Is it cold there? Do you like it? Have you travelled before? Do you have any brothers or sisters? What do your parents do? Where are they from? After I answered each question Masako had another one ready. I responded, but was wary of divulging too much. Since the failure of my romantic air-drop, my plan was to lie low, waiting out the two months required before activating my open ticket and flying home. Until then I only wanted to read and float around town, like a ghost on a clunky bicycle.

But when Masako broached my interests, I told her, with no small amount of pride, that I enjoyed the novels of Haruki Murakami and Banana Yoshimoto, remembering to exchange their first and last names as I spoke them.

"Modern authors," she said, her interrogation finally stalled. She recognized the names, but they meant nothing to her.

"Modern authors," I replied, blushing. She wasn't interested in books. Not long after, she excused herself to go to the bathroom, and I snuck out without saying goodbye.

⋮ Weeks passed before I saw Masako again. One day I came home from the library and found a message on the answering machine. "Mr. Jeffrey, you are leaving Japan soon and we must meet. Please call Masako," was followed by the digits of a telephone number.

I let the message sit for a day or two. I was sure I wouldn't reply, but didn't know why.

In Japan, shyness gripped the most unlikely candidates. At home, my ex was an extrovert, but here she was silenced by an unfamiliar language and a national obsession with etiquette. She rode her bike to work through the rainy season rather than humiliate herself by inquiring about bus routes, and then nursed a cold for months instead of navigating the local hospital in her second language.

Before my arrival it had been hard for me to understand the weird feeling of alienation she described to me on the phone. But now I felt it, too. Masako's curiosity about me, not visitors to Japan from the West, or North Americans generally, but *me*—a Canadian, born 1979 in Ottawa, the country's capital, to a father in the civil service and mother from the rural north of the province—was somehow unbearable.

She persisted.

Our first outing was to the Kikkoman soy sauce factory in adjacent Chiba Prefecture. It was a warm January day, and the sun hung at an angle that seemed far too bright for the time of year. The factory's exposed metal tubes and cisterns gleamed. Inside, we were led into a large empty auditorium. House lights dimmed, and the Kikkoman story began, narrated in English as Masako had requested. The rise of the noble family firm into a multinational food industry giant was professionally told. The film ended with an uninspiring aerial shot of the company's Wisconsin plant, a long, flat, rectangular building.

A Japanese-speaking tour guide led us down wide hallways, insisting we peer through windows revealing the stages of production. Masako tapped at her portable translator, trying to find words in English to adequately describe the fermentation of soy beans. I smiled at everything she said. It was exhausting.

⋮ Two weeks later, I waited in front of my ex's apartment building, watching my white breath rise in the cool February air. At exactly 10:30, Masako's car pulled up next to the sidewalk. Sitting on the passenger side, Miyuki was taller than Masako, and her English more accomplished and casual. I shook her hand through the rolled-down window, noticing that she didn't bow. Getting in the back seat behind her, I saw patches of white in her short black hair.

They took me to a traditional craft shop. The quiet room was filled with ordered rows of exquisite objects: earthenware mugs, handmade papers, ceramic bowls, chopsticks made of delicate wood. The shelves near the door were lined with white porcelain cats of various sizes wearing inscrutable expressions and holding up their left paws. I chose a gold and red greeting card embossed with a drawing of one of these waving cats to send to my grandmother. It was the fanciest thing I could find under a thousand yen.

"Maneki Neko," the cashier said.

"Kawaii, ne?" I managed. Cute.

⋮ We sped to lunch through the narrow streets of a nearby village. On the threshold of a small home, Masako and Miyuki introduced me to their friends, the Tamakis. They bowed at us from the step above as we slipped out of our shoes. For lunch they served miso soup, rice balls, and, surprisingly, dainty cucumber sandwiches.

The Tamakis told me they had travelled the world, and although they had never visited the city I grew up in, they had certainly heard of it. After the food was cleared away by his wife, Mr. Tamaki produced the photo albums documenting their trips to Indonesia, Thailand, Italy, Hawai'i. At every destination a picture had been taken of Mrs. Tamaki wearing a floppy hat and standing next to a tour bus.

Now that they were too old to travel, they enjoyed the company of foreigners, he explained, producing a photo album lined with snapshots of pale young men and a few women. As I flipped the pages, they named the nationalities of their former guests: American, Australian, New Zealander, and even an Englishman. Some of the subjects looked surprised, but most smiled broadly and made the hand symbol that I understood as "peace," but in Japan means simply, "I am posing for a photograph." Shortly thereafter, when Mr. Tamaki took my photograph, I smiled and said, "Chizu."

When the flash went off, I wondered, not for the first time, what I was doing here. Not just in Japan or in the Tamaki's bright kitchen, but in my strange friendship with Masako, two decades my senior. Where were Masako and Miyuki's husbands, and why did these women want to spend time with me instead of with their families? It must have been simple kindness, as natural as anything else, but I still didn't understand it. In conversation with Masako, Miyuki, and the Tamakis, I found myself drifting, losing touch with myself and generalizing my life as I discussed it. I told them I worked at an art gallery, which was true enough, although my position at the city art facility was actually at the front desk, unlocking and locking the gallery door. I had never thought of myself as a model Canadian specimen, but here I was, dutifully answering questions about my country, the wilderness, the Rocky Mountains, Prince Edward Island, Toronto. Explaining that Niagara Falls was a little too far from Vancouver for a daytrip.

Masako hadn't known where to take me when I suggested that the next stop on our itinerary should be to nature. A park or a forest, I explained. After a quick discussion with Miyuki in Japanese, she backed the car out of the Tamakis' driveway.

I heard distant bird songs when I opened the car door. The nature preserve was an acre of trees behind a cemetery, across the street from a cowboy-themed convenience store. As we walked the rough gravel trail looping through sickly conifers, Masako admitted that she had never been here before, but that it was very pretty. The sun was now dimming in the west while yellow and red birds flitted by. I asked her their names. Masako pulled out her handheld translator, but I waved it away and asked her to say their names in Japanese. I repeated Masako's words as Miyuki politely corrected her identification of the red one. The day's strong sun had loosened the grip of the winter frost so that I could almost smell the soil beneath.

On the drive to the park, Miyuki had turned and spoken to me through the space between the two front seats. She told me she had lived for a time in Illinois, near Lake Michigan, and knew about the joys of nature. There wasn't much of it left in Japan, she said. Now, walking beside me down the gravel path, Miyuki turned to me and asked if I had a favourite bird.

"The loon," I answered.

"Loon?" she asked.

"A black and white water bird that sings strangely," I said. "With red eyes."

I raised my voice, screeching "Ha-oo-oo!" in a poor imitation of its call.

Masako's and Miyuki's eyes widened. Then, after a long pause, they began to laugh.

I explained that the song of a real loon lifted high above my limited range, before howling again.

As we neared the parking lot, I told them about the loon family in the lake near my family's cottage, and how, as a child, I was convinced that the same loons returned each year, just like we did.

"Maybe so," Masako said.

"Maybe," I said, and tried my call for the last time.

After driving five minutes into the darkening evening on narrow roads empty of traffic, Miyuki sat up straight in her seat. "I know that bird," she said. "The...loon?" I nodded as she explained how she once saw one in a film.

"It is a very beautiful bird," she said, and began explaining it to Masako in Japanese.

Crosswalk

JENNIFER HOULE

It's not a busy city. Our sidewalks are capacious, we've got room.
You could go a lifetime without bumping heads. Without

being required to circumvent. There are no hidden triangles, no
    isometric gaffes.
Nothing is oblique, here. Nothing is acute. I saw you on Main Street,

and I turned. Whatever happened to revolving doors? Our banks
are vulgar, they just squat there, vestibular vultures, slotted,
rounding corners.

Your face was not expressionless. I thought I saw a question
form and deliquesce, like: if we loitered on a sinkhole would
    we plummet

to the burrows that connect us, underground, or could we dangle
from the girders long enough to be discovered, snarled in cobwebs,

as it were? The way is open, much too open. What's happened
to porticoes, and what's become of fire escapes? In 1906,

this city burned. And it was swamp, once. I saw you on Main Street
and I turned, abandoned a trajectory I thought was absolute.

LORNA CROZIER

Watching
My Lover

I watch him hold his mother
as she vomits into a bowl.
After, he washes her face
with a wet cloth and we try
to remove her soiled gown
tied in the back with strings.

Unable to lift her
I pull the green cotton
from under the blankets, afraid
I'll tear her skin.
He removes the paper diaper.
No one has taught us
how to do this, what to say.
Everything's so fragile here
a breath could break you.

She covers her breasts with hands
bruised from tubes and needles,
turns her face away.
It's okay, Mom, he says.
*Don't feel shy. I've undressed
dozens of women in my time.*
In this room where my lover
bares his mother, we three laugh.

Later, I curl naked beside him
in our bed, listen to his sleeping,
breath by breath. So worn out

he burns with fever—the fires
his flesh lights to keep him
from the cold.

Though he has washed
I smell her on his skin
as if she has licked him
from head to toe
with her old woman's tongue
so everyone who lies with him
will know he's still
his mother's son.

BEN GELINAS

Other People's Agony

AN OLD MAN HAD A HEART ATTACK as he drove down a quiet
stretch of highway a few years back. Dying behind the wheel,
he launched his truck through a fence, deep into a farmer's
field, where it settled in a spot not quite visible from the road.
Strapped to the car seat in the back was his grandson. The little
boy died of heatstroke before police found the truck.

Another time, someone backed over a two-year-old girl while
she played, unattended, in an apartment parking lot. The driver
took off, leaving her parents to find her body. It happened during
a yard sale. Her parents only lost sight of her for a minute.

How I made a living interviewing the families of these poor
kids I'll never know.

When I was in university, just starting journalism school, I had
a nervous breakdown just facing my classmates.

We were a small group at the University of Regina's Journalism
School—only about twenty-eight of us. We'd competed for a chance
to study there, clearing a combination of tests and interviews
with the department professors. I felt pretty lucky to get in, and
immediately decided I didn't deserve it. I assumed my classmates
were all bound for foreign bureaus and national newscasts, and
that I was a seventh-round pick, reluctantly selected because ten
more-qualified applicants got into superior schools like Carleton
and Ryerson.

One of the only people I recognized in the class was a twenty-
something political science grad named Adam Hunter. I knew
him through his girlfriend, who worked with me at a local Italian
restaurant. I didn't really get along with Adam back then. I think it
had something to do with his assuming I was trying to steal his
girlfriend away from him.

Also, I was trying to steal his girlfriend away from him.

By the time we both entered journalism school, they had broken up. And for all that we both scoffed at her for insisting we would "get along," it turned out we actually did.

Adam, the kind of booming personality destined for TV, sat next to me, and we paired up for our first assignment: interview one of our peers and present the findings to the rest of the class.

The professor told us to start broad and focus on whatever interesting angle we dug up.

Adam asked me a bunch of questions about my background: where I went to high school, what I did for fun. Then he zeroed in on my life growing up with divorced parents. This was fine. I liked to joke about how my family was broken, how being the only child of four parents, with all its negatives, at least meant twice as many toys come Christmas.

The next day, we took turns presenting our findings to the class. I think we sat in chairs at the front of the class, like we were on television, though maybe I'm remembering it wrong, and we actually stayed at our desks. Whatever the set-up, our presentation did not go well. As I listened to Adam tell our new classmates about how easy it is to get your dad to buy you a Sega Genesis when your mom's living with some other guy, I started to imagine what awful things all these people in front of us might be thinking. I immediately decided they were all judging me, probably thinking I was weak, maybe manipulative, probably a loser.

And I freaked. In the middle of Adam's presentation, I stood up and walked out of the classroom, muttering, "Keep going. It's fine." All eyes were trained on me as I left.

There was a washroom on the other side of the humanities building, where I hid in a stall for what must have been half an hour, certain I ruined my chances of ever gaining the respect of these handsome people I was to spend the next two years studying with.

Adam was left alone at the front of the class to finish the presentation without me.

"I was like: 'What the fuck did I say?'" he recalls. "I remember thinking you were an attention whore."

The funny thing is, walking out actually seemed to endear me to my classmates. Sure, they thought I was weird. But I guess it made me approachable.

And they absolutely knew who I was after that.

My lack of a spine proved a serious liability with the assignments, though. All through school I grappled with interviewing, especially. I was terrified to question strangers, and stumbled through the most basic interviews, feeling much the same way I had felt during Adam's presentation. In later assignments, I couldn't run away. I would have failed.

"Hi. Um...I'm Ben. Can I ask you some questions? Oh, I'm a reporter. In training. Sorry. I guess I should have said that first. I'm working on something for school. Could I ask you some questions? You don't have to answer anything you don't feel like answering."

I'd recite the most basic questions—the whos and the whats—ten times before dialing a phone number, only to have these questions fly out of my head the moment someone picked up. They were often replaced with awkward pauses. I developed a crippling fear of Jr. B hockey players and small-town nannies. No amount of practice improved my skills.

Somehow, I was still able to get an internship at the *Edmonton Journal*, an actual newspaper, on the back of a handful of anthropology papers and an interview with the manager editor, during which I focussed heavily on bashing tabloids.

The *Journal* newsroom was way scarier than journalism school. To survive that first step through the door, I told myself I'd go in, ask a ton of questions, and soak up everything I could. Mistakes would be inevitable, but I'd learn from them. Maybe I'd even get over my fear of interviewing when faced with the real thing.

They sat me near this workhorse of an investigative reporter named Chuck Rusnell, a senior writer who was also a Regina graduate. In my first week, he pulled me aside and told me he'd been listening to my interviews.

They were awful, he said.

I explained that I was nervous. It was like going on stage and forgetting the lines now that there was a proper audience.

Chuck said he'd solved a similar problem. He told me to write out what I was going to say before every interview, no matter how minor, including the preamble.

"Hi. My name is Ben Gelinas. I'm a reporter with the *Edmonton Journal*," he told me to type. Then he said to write out five key questions that needed to be asked. Any time I tripped up or got nervous, I could fall back on this script.

It was a simple thing that worked wonders. I started drafting a script every time I had an interview, no matter how inconsequential. If I interviewed someone in person, I would fill the first page of my notebook with the same preamble and five questions.

When I became a crime reporter, this script was how I survived.

Writing about death was the last thing I wanted to do. Not that I minded the scene work. Walking around crime scenes in search of witnesses made me feel like a bit of a gumshoe.

I liked looking for leads. And the gory stuff didn't really bother me.

I can't count how many times I got fresh blood on the soles of my shoes for not watching where I walked at a stabbing scene.

The dead were usually covered with a tarp or otherwise concealed by the time the reporters arrived. But there were exceptions. Sometimes the bodies were left uncovered to preserve evidence, eyes agape, top lip curled up, stiffening in the sun or cold. One young man in the driver's seat of a nice import took what looked like six bullets to his left side while waiting at a red light. From the edge of the tape, you could count the holes in his head. His body stayed behind the wheel for hours while the cops processed the scene, its hands stuck at ten and two, the car still running but frozen in place as the light changed from red to green to red again. When the medical examiner pulled the body from the car, its hands stayed out in front, as if still gripping that wheel.

No matter how recent the death, the victims always looked empty, like something had flittered off and left a shell of a person. They were like mannequins. We were even taught not to call victims "him" or "her" in print, but to instead write "his or her body."

It was the families they left behind that bothered me. I fretted extensively over interviews with people who wanted to talk to me. Now I regularly reached people on the worst days of their lives. Every time someone died under criminal circumstances, the job required me to find and try to interview those closest to them.

I tried to put off these interviews as much as possible. Once I found a phone number or address, I took a second, or minute, to collect myself. It was absolutely terrifying. I could ruin already ruined lives if I said the wrong thing, and I was the kind of guy who always said the wrong thing.

I did my best to minimize the trauma such an interview might inflict. My scripts always started with something that wouldn't immediately make them hang up, like, "I'm sorry to have to reach you like this, but I'm writing about what happened to your brother. I need to make sure my report is accurate. And I wanted to give you the opportunity to share your thoughts."

The vulnerable person on the other end of the phone also needed to know that I was a reporter as soon as possible. It's a special kind of unethical to pretend you're not a journalist when trying to get information out of the grieving father, mother, or friend of a dead man. The word "reporter" in particular needed to get way up front. I can't tell you the number of times people, grieving or not, heard "newspaper" and said, "We already subscribe, thanks," before hanging up.

I always started with the least controversial questions, purposefully avoiding anything that would hint at death until I'd nailed down a proper biography of the victim. I asked who the dead man was, what he did for a living, and what he meant to those who knew him best. Often, I would get the same answers over and over. A dead man was always kind to everyone, or in the case of more a troubled dead man, always turning his life around. Follow-up questions were often required. I needed concrete examples of how he was kind and how he was turning his life around. I wanted to know the victim as well as possible, so I could understand the full impact of the death.

Only after I built up trust did I start into the more difficult questions: What happened? Why?

These questions were much more likely to upset the person on the other end of the phone. It was always better, if possible, to talk in person. But usually this was impossible. People are hard to reach and hard to count on. If I had them talking, it was best to let them finish.

Sometimes they would burst into tears without warning. That was bad. Worse, though, was accidentally reaching a mother, or father, or brother before the police did. I was not trained to do a proper next of kin notification like the cops or doctors. I'm not sure if there's a way to train for it.

I kept a special script prepared for the rare times it happened, which I based on advice from past cop reporters. I gave the shocked family member the number to the homicide section and got off the phone as quickly as possible. They could call me back if they wanted, but I suggested they do so only after they dealt with the important things.

Every interview was like defusing a bomb. I worded my questions with the utmost care. And I never asked, "How do you feel?" Because, really, how do you think they felt?

I inevitably felt like a monster every time I picked up the phone. But I felt worse writing stories when I wasn't able to reach a family member.

There was one story involving a highway pursuit by RCMP. A man stole a van in the mountain town of Jasper and was speeding the wrong way down a busy stretch of road. Police followed until he reached a hill. The innocent driver on the other side couldn't have seen the van barreling toward him. The two men hit head-on. Both burned in the fire.

We were quick to get the name of the innocent man. His family was ready to talk because they were angry.

The name of the man fleeing from police was harder to track down. The burnt body meant RCMP at first had trouble identifying him. And when they finally confirmed it, they issued a release that simply said they wouldn't be telling anyone his name out of respect for the family.

Out of respect for the innocent man's family, I started looking for the name. A call to the medical examiner confirmed it. And I started dialing. I called everyone listed with his last name in

Alberta and neighbouring provinces. I dug around on Facebook for anyone who could be related, sending messages to all of them, being purposely vague, just saying that I was looking for his relatives. Nothing worked. All I confirmed by the end of the day was his name, and we had to go with it. The short story ran on a back page of the paper:

> The medical examiner has identified the second man killed in a RCMP chase near Hinton earlier this month.
>
> Stephen Kenyon, 21, was behind the wheel of a stolen van that collided with an oncoming pickup truck as he sped the wrong way down the Yellowhead with RCMP cruisers in pursuit.
>
> Kenyon was also wanted at the time of the crash on an outstanding warrant for shoplifting.
>
> The collision killed Brad Kerfoot, 30, the driver of the pickup truck.
>
> The crash is still under investigation by the Alberta Serious Incident Response Team, which investigates incidents involving officers that lead to serious injury or death.

The next morning, a woman called me, hysterical and sobbing so loudly into the receiver that all I could hear was static. Between breaths, she asked me where I got off publishing her fiancé's name, because, really, what right did I have?

I took a deep breath before calmly apologizing to the poor woman. I explained that I had tried to reach her, that the last thing I wanted was to run a story like that.

"You don't know him," she cried. "You don't know him."

I wanted to run away.

"Tell me about him," I said instead, surprising myself.

She went quiet for a moment, then whispered, "You really want to know?"

"Yes," I said.

"Can you come over now?" she asked.

"Yes," I said.

I drove over to her friend's house, where she was staying with her son—Kenyon's son. She answered the door, her face a raw red, her eyes at the floor. We sat on a couch and stared at the white wall in front of us as we talked. She told me Kenyon was a good father and a hard worker who helped his brother with his roofing business. Then she told me he had shared troubling thoughts with her in the months before his death. She said he feared he was going crazy and he didn't know what to do. Periodically, we stopped the interview so she could cry a little or attend to her son, who would wander into the room, oblivious. Then she put me on the phone with Kenyon's brother, who was up on a roof when we talked.

The next day, I wrote a long piece about the man and the family he left behind. I never spoke with them again. I often wonder what they thought of it.

The nervous tone and pregnant pauses that were once inevitable byproducts of my shyness became byproducts of the guilt I felt for having the gall to make these calls.

Strangely, my disposition worked to set the poor people at ease. The worse I felt, the more they seemed to open up.

When someone answered the phone, the tone of my voice went pillow-soft. I spoke slowly and quietly, and didn't hide the guilt, apologizing not for their loss, but for the rudeness of reaching them to talk about it.

I had to live with myself. And at its core, the job of a crime reporter is morally questionable. The line between the public interest and the exploitation of grief doesn't seem to exist.

I ultimately decided if I didn't do it, someone else would. And that someone might not treat the people on the other end of the line as delicately as I did.

After hundreds of these interviews, though, the pressure got to be too heavy. I started lashing out at my friends, coworkers, family, and my poor girlfriend at the time. She was good to me, stayed up with me so many nights as I paced around the house wondering if I'd gotten the tiniest detail wrong in the next day's homicide story. Sometimes I puked myself hoarse on account of the heartburn. I was convinced I had an ulcer.

I felt personally responsible for the grief of these families. I knew I was contributing to it. And knowing this made the interviews harder and harder.

The stabbing death of one north-side drug dealer in particular broke me. The homicide cops eventually declared his death non-culpable. The details were vague. But it seemed he brought it on himself in some way. It may have been self-defence.

The police said they didn't have a case.

When his fiancée was called into police headquarters to be told the file would be closed without charges, someone tipped off the TV reporters, who camped outside, waiting for her to come out. When she emerged, they asked her what happened. She began to sob there on the sidewalk as the cameras filmed.

Later that day, I sat with this woman at her kitchen table in a dingy basement apartment. She told me about the phone calls she'd been getting. People were calling her up to say her fiancé deserved what he got. She wondered if they knew he had a kid.

In the middle of our interview, the news came on in the living room. She stopped talking and turned to the TV. As she watched herself cry on camera, she broke down at the table in front of me, drowning out the previously recorded breakdown on display to the whole city at six.

I stared at my hands. Our photographer snapped a photo of her.

In those hellish moments, collecting intimate details from broken strangers, I was absorbed by their agony. My once-crippling shyness no longer mattered. I forgot to be shy. I was able to completely step outside of myself, because, for once, it wasn't about me. It was about them—their thoughts, emotions, and loss. I was just an interpreter, charged with relaying an unimaginable grief to curious strangers. But what good did it do? Hundreds of interviews brought me no closer to justifying the job. No amount of rationalizing trumped the guilt that constantly haunted me. Eventually, I quit, found a job editing dialogue for video games set in a fantasy world.

Many reporters assigned to cover crime in major cities are in their early twenties, like I was. The few senior reporters who remain in city newsrooms rarely want to cover crime. So the business inevitably feeds off young, cheap blood.

Sometimes I wonder how the new kids on the crime beat are faring. The eager or not-so-eager interns, fresh out of J-school. The Type A twenty-somethings who love the camera. I picture some young reporters I knew, the ones who had no problem rolling the camera while knocking on the door of a victim's house without warning. I wish I could tell them to just be a little more shy, that maybe it helps.

WADE BELL

It's Okay
that Late at Night

It's okay that late at night the narrow unmade bed
the birthmark of bitter wine in the valley of the glass
the musicians exiting though the window

It's all right to worry that the daily bread will go stale
the water evaporate like the image in the photograph
to want foreign fingers with caresses like magma

rising through sand all right to dream the smell of morning
in the tropics to spend life at both ends of the microscope
It's okay to need lessons in breathing

All right to send tears to comfort the lost breast
to cool the amputated psyche fog self-consciousness
dilute the shame grown Hollywood monstrous

from a Petri dish of childhood rebukes and ridicule
for the step too far for the word too many
The chair rocked back eventually rocks forward

Daughter of Atlas Maia lived in a cave avoiding company
Zeus exploring the shadowed mountains
discovered her and wooed her in secret

In secret she entertained him
in secret gave birth to Hermes
son of love and the fiery passion

that is the secret of the shy
To hide the stain refill the glass
Will the image back to the photo

Shout the word take the step
Liberate the word take many steps
long full steps will take you far

DEBBIE BATEMAN

Amongst the Unseen and Unheard

IT WORKS BEST in a pine-scented forest or on a dusty country road in the new light of morning. If I manage to remain unnoticed, I spot the wide-eyed deer in the brush, or the coyote skulking in the hay field. I take my glimpse and move on with hushed breath.

I can do it in a city park if I have to. Running through the shadows of poplar trees or next to the rushing river, I step lightly so passers-by won't notice me. Dark sunglasses and a long-billed running cap add to my disguise. A light snow is welcome because it blurs my features. A stiff wind is useful too, the kind that flings hair over other people's eyes and makes them tuck their chins.

For as long as I can remember, I've practised being unseen and unheard. All through my childhood, I escaped my large family by going on solitary walks at our weekend farm. I liked to bury myself in tall grass by the beaver pond, raising the collar of my flannel shirt over my head to keep away bugs. The sun warmed my clothes, and the mossy earth was gentle beneath me. Listening to the trills of red-winged black birds or the faraway ticking of a woodpecker, I found refuge. In winter, I lay on the snow-covered ground. Wearing snow pants for warmth, I disappeared into the vastness of a deserted field. Puffs of white skidded over the icy surface around me, while I stared into the wide blue sky. The cold air held a special kind of silence.

It takes more effort amongst people, but it can be done. On the last day of high school when everyone else celebrated with their friends, I sat alone in the schoolyard under a tree and wrote a poem. It's in my yearbook. I put it there a few weeks after high school was over, along with the signatures of friends that fill the blank pages at the front and back. The poem ends like this: "Remembering and sometimes forgetting, and knowing that I go as I came, surrounded by people but nevertheless alone."

⋮ I could claim it's because I need time to think, that I don't like to speak before I know what I'm talking about. I could say I prefer listening. There's so much to learn by remaining silent. Subtext is revealed to those able to pay attention. Most people are too concerned with their own ideas to notice the slight raising of an eyebrow, the curling of a lip, or the sneer beneath the surface of the skin. I see it all, and as a result can foretell with startling accuracy the ending of a love relationship or an impending clash of wills between colleagues.

A nicer justification for my reserved attitude might be that it attracts the best sort of friends. Patient and soft-spoken, only the gentlest souls, deeply sensitive and kind to the bone, are willing to wait for me to emerge. It can take weeks or months or years, depending on the degree of pressure. The less I am forced, the more likely I am to step forward.

My hesitant nature makes it easy for me to adjust to others who also need time to forge human connections. Because I recognize and respect the limits of shy people, I make friends extroverts never will. I used to work next to a woman who rarely spoke, yet every morning she greeted me with an unrestrained smile, and I returned the gesture.

We didn't need large volumes of words to establish friendship. The exchange of smiles led to spurts of verbal communication, which turned into coffee-break walks, then grew into outings for lunch and the occasional supper together in a vegetarian restaurant. Sharing with one another our personal histories and mutual fear of social situations, we formed a bubble of calm in an otherwise chaotic cubicle farm. In one another's company, we found unconditional acceptance, a rare gift for shy people. So many would rather fix us than understand us.

She made my work life distinctly better, but it makes me sad sometimes when I think about it now. Most people will never know that she designs and sews all her own clothes, that she has a passion for world travel, or that she gently nurtures and protects the fifty orchids growing in her home. Each flower needs a slightly different temperature, degree of sunlight, and amount of water.

⋮ I could say all those things, and they would be true, but they would cover up the basic reality. A lot of the time, it's raw fear, the worst kind imaginable. The kind that grips the back of my throat and makes my pulse roar. The kind that drains every coherent thought from my head and makes my body quake. When it happens, I dread looking the way I feel, so utterly foolish and stupid.

As research for a work project, I once took an Instructional Skills Workshop. The idea was to learn enough about effective teaching to script a video for continuing education instructors. A key element of the workshop was what they called mini-lessons. Each of us had to create a series of ten-minute lessons and deliver them in a small group. Compared to teaching a full-length class of thirty students, this was a minor exercise for most of the participants.

For me, it was terrifying. The first time I tried to deliver a ten-minute lesson, I lost all the moisture in my mouth. I couldn't focus on a single object. The room became a nauseating swirl of colours. I could hardly form words; yet, strangely, no one seemed to notice the depth of my anxiety. Each time I gave a lesson, it was less distressing. By the final one, I could glimpse the faces of my group members, provided I didn't linger. But I never reached the point where I could stand in front of them and speak spontaneously. The best I could do was recite a carefully worded speech. The instructor said it sounded like I was reading from a text, and she was right. Although I had no papers in hand, I conjured the printed words in my head to guide me.

Months later, in an evening course, I wrote a script for a dramatic short and had to pitch the story in front of the class. We were a small and friendly group. Our teacher had been a professional comedian, so the atmosphere tended to be lighthearted and silly. It seemed like the perfect opportunity to experiment with thinking on my feet. Although I organized my thoughts beforehand, for once I didn't arrange them into a speech.

I did better than ever before. More than a minute passed without incident. I stood at the front of the room with a normal amount of moisture in my mouth and a body that was not trembling. It seemed like everything was going to be okay. Then I looked at the intense focus on my classmates' faces, and all of a sudden I had a full-out systems crash in my brain. I couldn't remember what I wanted to say, or even what had just come out of my mouth.

My eyes remained glued to their expectant faces. While they waited for me to continue, nervous tension buzzed through my guts. It formed a prickly ball that tumbled inside me, gradually growing until it burst wide open, filling my chest with a tingling sense of panic. I would've liked to turn away. I would've liked to run. But I stood there, a quivering mute. And then the instructor rescued me. "If you can't think of anything else, just give them a smile and say, that's my story."

I returned to my seat, and life moved on. The next person gave his pitch, then the person after that. The instructor made useful comments, and I concentrated on listening. Soon my breathing returned to normal. Halfway through class we took our usual break, everyone gathering in the hall the same way we'd done since the first night we'd met. People talked to me, looking straight at my face. They didn't turn their heads and cover their mouths to suppress barely audible snickers. They laughed as much as they always did, but never once did anyone laugh at me.

To this day, I can be choked silent by social anxiety. It has happened a few times since that moment in front of the class, although in less noticeable ways. But having my worst fear realized did loosen its grip a little, and for that I am grateful. All my life I'd lived in dread of just that kind of moment. Then it actually happened, and I was astonished to discover how insignificant it was. Although I was embarrassed, the awkwardness only lasted minutes. Once I'd survived, I had to admit the whole thing had been founded on an inflated sense of my own importance.

The most damaging part of shyness isn't the embarrassment. It's the missed opportunities that accumulate, all the moments when I could have made meaningful connections but failed because I was afraid. Over the years, I've stood in countless lines waiting for favourite authors to sign my copy of their books. Usually, I'm wearing a jacket in an overly heated theatre. A slick of sweat has formed on the back of my neck. My face is flushed, and I can hardly breathe at the thought of meeting a person I greatly admire.

While I watch other people chatting comfortably with the author, I run through possible comments in my head, eventually throwing out every last one because none seems adequate for describing the book I hold in my hand. Afterwards, I hate myself for not coming forward, for not encouraging the author's hard work, for not showing the world what matters to me. It's not good enough to formulate coherent sentences half an hour later. I need to speak in the moment. What if that author might have shared something important about writing? What if I missed the perfect tip, the secret trick of the trade, the one piece of skill or understanding that could take my own work to a deeper level?

David Adams Richards is amongst the authors I admire most. In particular, I'm fascinated by *Mercy Among the Children*. The novel conveys the complexity of a community, all of its struggle: the misdirected attempts at kindness, the thinly veiled animosity, and the noble virtue of a quiet man steadfastly refusing to beg the truth. The author raises deep moral questions. He tells a personal story of universal importance. Yet when I had a chance to talk to him, I wasted it.

Timidly, I handed him my copy of his book, mumbling my name and making him ask me to repeat it. With downcast eyes and a soft voice, he seemed almost as shy as I was. I watched him open the cover of my well-worn copy, hoping he'd notice the softened edges of the paper, the pages that had been turned repeatedly.

He'd finished signing, had placed the book in my hand, and was looking toward the next person in line before I finally said something. "I enjoyed your book so much, when I reached the end, I flipped it back to the beginning and started over." Although my voice was louder than usual, it was still not easily heard.

Thinking he was too busy with the next person to notice me, I continued moving away, but at the sound of his voice, my head turned.

"Thank you, Debbie," he said.

⋮ Shyness is a cage. It traps me inside its silence. I can't get out, and other people can't get in. If the walls were thick and solid, it might be tolerable, even comforting, to be in the company of my own thoughts. The cage might be as familiar as the flannel shirt over my head when I was a child at rest on mossy ground by the beaver pond. But I'm an adult, now. There are no walls on my cage, only bars. Through the openings, I see everything I'm missing, and I torture myself trying to understand why others do not always seem able to see me.

Throughout my life, I have been passed over. When neighbourhood kids gathered in the field, no one picked me for their baseball team. At school dances, I waited against the cement wall as guys approached the girls next to me. I have been overlooked in my career multiple times: not considered for interesting projects, not included in team recognition, skipped over in favour of people with more outgoing personalities.

I can be with a close friend, yet hesitate to speak so long, an entire hour passes in utter monologue, my only contribution the occasional *uh-huh* or nod. In a year of regularly attending a yoga studio, I can fail to make a single acquaintance. At a party, I can sit on a couch between two women chatting happily around me as if I weren't there, never including me in their conversation. They can continue talking several hours, while I fade into non-existence, too scared to get up and go somewhere else where people might notice I am alive and breathing. Afterwards, in the darkened car on the drive home with hot tears wetting my cheeks, I vow never to allow myself to be so invisible again.

⋮ As part of my self-prescribed aversion therapy, I go to a bar on Saturday afternoons with my husband, to listen to jazz and practise the art of making conversation. I love the music and could happily sit there for the three hours just listening. The people surrounding me might even let me get away with that. We are all there primarily for the music, but I also encourage myself to talk to people.

We've been attending for more than five years, and for the first two I felt such anxiety an hour before leaving the house, I'd start to tense. My shoulders would rise. My jaw would clamp down. I'd hear the heartbeat blasting in my ears, sense the quiver coming into my breath, and tell myself to stop getting worked up over nothing. When admonitions didn't help, I'd move on to inquisition. What was I worried about? Why was I anxious? I never found answers. The fear was dark and deep, and refused to explain itself. By the time we'd arrive, every muscle in my body would be clenched. I was unsure of my ability to safely cross the room. As the saxophone riffed, I caught myself gripping the sides of my chair, and not because of the music. Later, back at home, I'd hurt all over from the tension.

Yet we kept going, and I set myself a simple goal. Each time, I challenged myself to speak to one person. I began with a quiet man who didn't know anyone, and happened to be sitting next to me. Both of us shy, our voices were so soft we had to lean in and pay close attention to hear one another. I asked if he was enjoying the music. Then I asked what he did for a living. Soon we discovered he worked with my cousin at the local hospital. All it took was three or four awkward questions, and we were engaged in conversation. I forgot to worry about what I said, he was so interesting. He was a photographer, and we discussed the importance of seeing light and shadows.

Over the weeks and months and years, I repeated this exercise and made a number of meaningful friendships. Although I no longer feel anxiety going to this event, since I know many of the people there, I still behave in a disappointingly anti-social fashion some of the time. People whose friendship I cherish will sit a few steps away, and I will struggle to work up the courage to leave my seat and go talk to them.

The strange thing is, in certain contexts, I'm not shy at all. Catch me running a race, volunteering with children, or travelling in a foreign country where I don't speak the language well, and you'd swear I'm an extrovert. Immersed in something that ignites my sense of creativity and adventure, I lose all sense of hesitancy. For a moment at least, I openly approach the world. Afterwards, I challenge myself to imagine a life constructed only of environments in which I feel inspired and at ease. Every time I find myself in a situation that frees me, I add it to the list. Being part of a female book club, taking swimming lessons with people I don't know, sharing a campfire with backcountry travellers, collaborating with a creative team I trust—there have been many moments that drew me outward.

I also take note of situations that make me withdraw. Overly male organizations, people in uniform, and authority figures can tighten my throat and render me silent. So do ceremonies with elaborate protocol and parties thrown by the ostentatiously wealthy. If I suspect I do not belong, I shrink into an unreachable part of my soul, casting a stern expression to warn people away. Not everyone picks up the signals. A gregarious colleague happened to catch me in full retreat one day. Instead of keeping her distance, she drew near and asked what was wrong. The best explanation I could offer was that I suffer from social anxiety.

But even in environments where I'd normally hesitate to speak, I will immediately step forward if I think unfairness has occurred. I will jump three organizational layers, walk into the office of the person with the most power, and speak my mind openly while others remain silent. Under those conditions, I have no need to prepare a carefully worded speech. I know what to say. Not that my efforts have ever made any difference. Although surprised by my sudden willingness to speak, and respectful of my point of view, the people in power tend not to take me seriously. Maybe they realize that once I leave their office, I will return to my quiet and co-operative self, never causing reason for concern again.

⋮ The act of writing holds that same urgency. When it's going well, I don't hesitate to expose my true thoughts; I simply write. Perhaps it's because I keep so much inside. When the floodgates open, the sudden rush of unedited thought clears everything in its path. It carries away self-doubt, replacing my normal state of low-level anxiety with an intoxicating mix of bravery and freedom. In such moments, I'd rather be writing than doing anything else. Even when the results are not especially good.

Given a choice, I'd write my life rather than speak it. I'd carry a miniature whiteboard and a supply of multi-coloured felt pens. If I didn't like what I'd written, I smudge it out with the side of my hand and try again. I'd use different colours for each mood and large print for important information.

I once took a course on writing by Aboriginal women, taught by Aruna Srivastava. With a fresh look on what should be taught and how it should be learned, she guided us toward a different kind of knowledge. Instead of sitting auditorium-style, we arranged our desks in a circle. Instead of writing essays, we kept journals and created group websites. Best of all, instead of merely reading the works of Aboriginal women, we met some.

For most of the class, I was my usual reticent self, listening as other students shared their ideas, only speaking when called upon to contribute to group work or asked a direct question. Then Marilyn Dumont read her poetry and drew me into her reverie. When a silenced voice breaks through, it resounds with a deeper tone, the fullness of the words increased by their prolonged denial. By the time they are released, the thoughts have become precisely pitched notes capable of infiltrating even the thickest mind. The whole world must stop and listen.

After reading her work, she drew us into a discussion about writing. She told us that her journals provided the foundation for most of her poetry. Their pages gave space to her growing ideas. She'd brought one along to show us. We watched her unfold the bound notebook and run a fingertip over a blank page. Sometimes entire poems were born there. They came into being on the thick paper with light blue lines, coaxed into existence by the purposeful act of writing.

When she asked if any of us kept a journal, I said that I did. Even though I'd been hiding the notebooks for years, taking comfort in the knowledge that my handwriting was too messy for anyone else to read, I came forward. I didn't care who knew. Suddenly, it no longer had to be a secret. When she asked why I wrote, I told her it was to know my voice and how to use it. I said that, until I'd started journaling, I hadn't realized I could have a say in my own life. I had no idea what I really thought or felt. When you're unseen and unheard, you can remain hidden even from yourself. The poetry I'd written as a teenager was little more than the faraway rumblings of a stranger. I was thirty before I owned my words.

During the break, I approached Marilyn Dumont. She was deep in discussion with Aruna, their voices animated and their expressions warm. As I quietly waited a few steps away for an appropriate moment to interrupt, the familiar anxiety brewed inside me. Moments earlier, I had been comfortable talking to her in front of the entire class; now I was terrified of asking her to sign my copy of her book. I almost backed away several times. I should have realized it didn't matter whether I had anything clever to say.

She asked my name, then inscribed the book, her pen moving over the title page, filling more space than I'd ever expected. I waited until I was out of sight before opening the cover. This is what she wrote: "It is a great loss to the world that we didn't know what our own voice sounded like until age thirty."

I stood outside the building where we held our class, a cold fall wind slapping my face as I read the inscription several times. A wad of grief stopped my throat. I understood she was right. And I was not alone amongst the unseen and unheard. I'd never been.

Contributors

RONA ALTROWS has won the W.O. Mitchell Book Prize and the Brenda Strathern Prize for her fiction. She is the author of two collections of short stories, *A Run On Hose* and *Key In Lock*. Her stories and personal essays have been published widely in literary magazines. She also writes articles on the art and craft of writing and works as a freelance book editor. She has served as Writer-in-Residence for the Calgary Public Library and the Alexandra Writers' Centre Society.

DEBBIE BATEMAN belongs to the secret cult of writers who wake in the small hours and write before the demands of the day can take away their creative energy. It started when her children were young and 4:00 A.M. was the only time she could be certain of privacy. Her sons are men now, but the habit has remained. She recently finished her first novel and is now working on a collection of linked short stories. She supports her creative work by editing and writing learning materials for educational institutions, emergency services organizations, and the oil industry.

WADE BELL is the author of *Tracie's Revenge* (2012), *No Place Fit for a Child* (2009), *A Destroyer of Compasses* (2003), all published by Guernica Editions, and *The North Saskatchewan River Book*, stories set in Edmonton and Jasper, published by Coach House Press. From Edmonton, he has lived in Ottawa, Barcelona and Vulpellach, Spain, and Calgary.

ALEX BOYD is a Toronto poet. His books are *Making Bones Walk* (2007) and *The Least Important Man* (2012).

JANIS BUTLER HOLM lives in Athens, Ohio, where she has served as Associate Editor for *Wide Angle*, the film journal. Her essays, stories, poems, and performance pieces have appeared in small-press, national, and international magazines. Her plays have been produced in the US, Canada, and England.

BRIAN CAMPBELL's most recent collection is *Passenger Flight* (Signature Editions, 2009). His work has appeared in numerous reviews, including *CV2*, *Prairie Fire*, *The New Quarterly*, and *The Saranac Review*. In 2006 he was shortlisted for the CBC Literary Award for Poetry; in 2011, he received a Canada Council grant toward the completion of his third collection. Campbell lives in Montreal. It particularly pleases him that "Women Friends," which he previously had been too shy to submit, has finally found a suitable print-home more than a quarter century after it was written.

WEYMAN CHAN, a finalist for the 2008 Governor General's Award for his second book of poetry, *Noise from the Laundry*, divides his time between writing, family, electron micrographs, and non-sequitur fluxes in spacetime, brought on by insomnia....Catfish. His latest book, *Chinese Blue*, is an auto-replicated biography that unsuccessfully exceeds the impersonal.

LORNA CROZIER's books have won the Governor General's, the Canadian Authors Association, and two Pat Lowther Awards. A member of the Royal Society of Canada and a Distinguished Professor at the University of Victoria, she has published fifteen poetry collections, the most recent *The Blue Hour of the Day: Selected Poems* and *Small Mechanics*. She has received three honourary doctorates for her contribution to Canadian literature, and in 2011 became an Officer of the Order of Canada. She has read her work around the world. A memoir, *Small Beneath the Sky*, was published by Greystone Books in 2009. Concurrently, a Spanish translation of her poems, *La Perspectiva del Gato*, was published by Trilce Ediciones in Mexico City. Her newest book, *The Book of Marvels: A Compendium of Everyday Things*, was one of the *Globe and Mail's* top 100 books of 2012.

MIKE DUGGAN is a poet of Anglo-Irish descent. Married to a drama teacher, he is proud father of triplets—twin girls and a boy—the amazing result of IVF. He works as manager of an electrical wholesale outlet and recently completed a degree in English with the Open University. His poems have appeared in *The Rialto*, *Poetry & Audience*, and *Magma*, and he is working toward his first collection.

BEN GELINAS is a writer and editor currently based in Edmonton. He worked for a handful of years as a crime reporter for the *Edmonton Journal*, while also dabbling in arts writing. He left newspapers in 2011 for work as a story and dialogue editor at Edmonton-based video-game company BioWare.

ELIZABETH GREENE has published two collections of poetry, *The Iron Shoes* (Hidden Brook, 2007) and *Moving* (Inanna, 2010). A third collection, *Understories*, is due out from Inanna in 2014. One of her poems was a finalist for the Descant/Winston Collins Prize in 2012. She has edited/co-edited five books, including *We Who Can Fly: Poems, Essays and Memories in Honour of Adele Wiseman* (Cormorant, 1997), which won the Betty and Morris Aaron Award for Best Scholarship on a Canadian Subject. She taught English at Queen's University in Kingston, Ontario, for many years. She lives in Kingston with her son and three cats.

VIVIAN HANSEN is a Calgary poet and activist. She has run poetry workshops for The John Howard Society and Inn from the Cold literacy initiatives, and for youth at risk. She has published the chapbooks *Never Call It Bird: The Melodies of AIDS* and *Angel Alley: Jack the Ripper's Victims*. Her poetry collection *Leylines of My Flesh* (Touchwood, 2002) explores the experiences of Danish immigrants. Hansen holds an MFA in creative writing from the University of British Columbia. She was the 2012 Writer-in-Residence for the Danish Canadian National Museum in Dickson, Alberta, and her book *A Bitter Mood of Clouds* is forthcoming from Frontenac House.

ELIZABETH HAYNES's writing has appeared in magazines including *Alberta Views*, *Room*, *The Capilano Review*, *The Malahat Review*, and *Prism* as well as anthologies, most recently *Walk Myself Home: An anthology to end violence against women* (Caitlin Press, 2010). She's won the Western Magazine Award for fiction, the American Heart Association Award for fiction, and the Jon Whyte essay competition, twice. Her short fiction collection, *Speak Mandarin Not Dialect* (Thistledown Press) was a finalist for the Alberta Book Awards. Haynes is a Speech-Language Pathologist at the Institute for Stuttering Treatment and Research (an institute of the University of Alberta).

STEVEN HEIGHTON's most recent books are *Workbook* (memos and dispatches on writing), *Patient Frame* (a poetry collection), and *Every Lost Country* (a novel). His 2005 novel, *Afterlands*, appeared in six countries; was a *New York Times Book Review* editors' choice; and was a best-of-year choice in ten publications in Canada, the US, and the UK. Heighton's poems and stories have appeared in many publications—including *London Review of Books*, *Poetry*, *Tin House*, *TLR*, *The Walrus*, and *Best English Stories*—and have received four gold National

Magazine Awards. He has also been nominated for the Governor General's Award and Britain's W.H. Smith Award.

JENNIFER HOULE's work has appeared in numerous publications including *The Antigonish Review, The Fiddlehead, Arc, Room, Prairie Fire, CV2*, and *Dandelion*. She was the recipient of the Writers' Federation of New Brunswick's 2011 Alfred G. Bailey Poetry Prize. She lives in Fredericton, New Brunswick.

I.B. (BUNNY) ISKOV is the founder of The Ontario Poetry Society. Her work has been published in several literary journals and anthologies. She has published two full poetry collections and many chapbooks. Her newest collection is *In a Wintered Nest*, published by Serengeti Press in the fall of 2013.

EVE S. KRAKOW is a writer, journalist, and translator. Her stories and essays have appeared in *lichen literary journal, Smithsonian Magazine, Cahoots, Quebec Heritage News,* and *Writings* (Volume Two), an anthology by the Montreal branch of the Canadian Authors Association. She lives in Montreal, Quebec, with her husband and two children.

SHAWNA LEMAY is a writer, blogger, editor, Getty Images artist, and library assistant. She is the creator and editor of the website *Canadian Poetries*. She resides in Edmonton with her partner, Robert Lemay, a visual artist, and their daughter, Chloe.

NAOMI K. LEWIS grew up in Ottawa and lives in Calgary. Her novel *Cricket in a Fist* was published in 2008, and she co-wrote Spencer Beach's bestselling 2010 memoir, *In Case of Fire*. Lewis was the 2011 Writer-in-Residence at the Calgary Public Library. Her 2012 story collection, *I Know Who You Remind Me Of*, won Enfield & Wizenty's Colophon Prize and was shortlisted for the Alberta Readers' Choice Award and the Georges Bugnet Award for Fiction.

SHIRLEY LIMBERT lived and wrote in Prince Edward Island. She told tales since she was quite small, and at fourteen wrote for *Tiny Tots*, a national children's magazine in England. In May 2001 she achieved a lifelong ambition and published a book of poems, *Lilacs Year to Year*. A book of creative non-fiction, *Seachange Cottage*, came out in April 2005. Her third book, *Melanie: A Love Story*, Limbert's first lesbian novel, was published in February 2007. Her poems, articles, and award-winning short stories have appeared in publications including *Our Lives, By Word of Mouth, Kaleidoscope, Island Moments, Tide Lines,* and *A Time of Trial: Beyond the Terror of 9/11*. Shirley Limbert died peacefully at home on June 10, 2013.

CAROL L. MACKAY is an introvert living on Vancouver Island. Her poems have been heard on CBC Radio and have recently appeared in *The Fiddlehead, Prairie Journal*, and *Existere*. Her introvert tendencies can keep her from actively participating in readings, but she does, on occasion, suck it up and present her work in public. Her closest friends don't believe she is shy.

MICHELINE MAYLOR's latest book, *Whirr and Click*, is available through Frontenac House. She teaches creative writing at Mount Royal University and edits *FreeFall Magazine* in Calgary. She thanks all the authors at Wordfest for inspiring her shyness poem.

DON MCKAY has written many books of poetry, including *Paradoxides* (2012), and several volumes of essays addressing wilderness poetics, including *The Shell of the Tortoise* (2011). He has received a number of awards, including the Governor General's Award, twice, and the Griffin Poetry Prize. He lives in St. John's, Newfoundland. "Sometimes a Voice (1)" appears in *Another Gravity* (2000).

STUART IAN MCKAY is a member of the Writers' Guild of Alberta and the League of Canadian Poets. He is a two-time winner of CBC's *Alberta Anthology*. *Stele of Several Ladies: a long poem*, his first book, was published in 2005. He lives in Calgary. "a more blissful orbit" is from a manuscript in progress and was set to music by resident musicians at the Banff Centre for the Arts in February 2010. McKay's newest book of poetry is *a cognate of prayer* (2013).

BRUCE MEYER is professor of English at Georgian College and the inaugural poet laureate for the City of Barrie. He is author or editor of thirty-four books of poetry, fiction, non-fiction, pedagogy, literary journalism, and emblemata. His most recent books are *Mesopotamia, Dog Days, Alphabet Table, Alphabestiary* (with H. Masud Taj), *The White Collar Book* (with Carolyn Meyer), and *A Book of Bread*.

JEFF MILLER is the author of the short-story collection *Ghost Pine: All Stories True* (Invisible Publishing, 2010). He lives in Montreal and spends his summers in Jeddore, Nova Scotia.

DHANA MUSIL is a 2011 graduate of The Writer's Studio at Simon Fraser University. Her creative non-fiction has won several awards and has been published in various newspapers and publications. She is currently working on her memoir, which chronicles the decade she spent living and loving in the underworld of Japan. Dhana lives in Vancouver with her partner, two daughters, and two cats.

LORI D. ROADHOUSE is a Calgary writer, poet, and aphorist. She founded the Hilltop Writers critiquing group, and co-created the 2003 Writing Toward the Light Poetry Contest/Concert. She is a member of the Writers' Guild of Alberta and the Alexandra Writers' Centre Society. Roadhouse is a board member of the Single Onion Poetry Society. From 2008 to 2010, she was co-artistic director, performer, and MC of Lotus Land at South Country Fair. She was the 2009 poet-in-residence for *Radiant Lights* E-Magazine. She is a featured reader at poetry and spoken word events, and has been published in many magazines, newsletters, websites, radio programs, CDs, and anthologies.

KERRY RYAN lives and writes in Winnipeg. Her first full-length collection of poetry, *The Sleeping Life*, was published by The Muses' Company in 2008 and shortlisted for the Aqua Books Lansdowne Prize for Poetry. Her second book, *Vs.*, a collection of poems about boxing, was published by Anvil Press in 2010 and was a finalist for the Acorn-Plantos Award for People's Poetry.

SYDNEY SHARPE is an award-winning, bestselling author of such books as *The Gilded Ghetto: Women and Political Power in Canada*; *Storming Babylon: Preston Manning and the Rise of the Reform Party* (with Don Braid), and *Staying in the Game: The Remarkable Story of Doc Seaman*. Her most recent book is *Seeking the Summit: Sam Switzer's Story of Building and Giving*. Educated at Calgary's Bowness High School, the University of Alberta, and McGill University, Sharpe was a tenured professor of anthropology and left academia to become a writer. She has been a senior columnist for the *Calgary Herald*, Calgary Bureau Chief for the *Financial Post*, and a press gallery member in Ottawa. Also, she's shy.

NATALIE SIMPSON's first book, *accrete or crumble*, was published by LINEbooks in 2006. Her poetry has also appeared in the anthologies *Shift & Switch* (Mercury) and *Post-Prairie* (Talonbooks). She is a former managing editor of *filling Station* magazine and intermittently publishes limited-edition chapbooks through her press, edits all over. She practises law in Calgary.

SYLVIA STOPFORTH is a university archivist and reference librarian whose fiction has appeared in *Room* and *TNQ*; she has also published work-related articles and book reviews, and serves as volunteer editor of a column in *BC History: The Journal of the British Columbia Historical Federation*. She lives with her husband in White Rock, BC.

DAVID VAN BUREN grew up in Westchester County, New York. He
graduated from SUNY at Oneonta, with a BS in English. Since the
mid-1970s, he's worked as an editor and writer for various companies
in both New York and Dublin—where he moved in 1991, and currently
lives with his wife and five children. Writing credits include poems
published in various journals, a weekly column ("An American In
Dublin") for the *Irish Voice Newspaper* (NYC), and a children's picture
book, *I Love You as Big as the World*, published in 2008 by Little Tiger
Press (London) and Good Books (USA).

ARITHA VAN HERK is the author of five novels: *Judith*, *The Tent Peg*,
No Fixed Address, *Places Far From Ellesmere* (a geografictione), and
Restlessness. Her critical work is collected in *A Frozen Tongue* and
In Visible Ink; she has published hundreds of articles, reviews, and
essays. *Mavericks: An Incorrigible History of Alberta* won the Grant
MacEwan Author's Award for Alberta Writing. That book frames the
Alberta history exhibition at the Glenbow Museum and Archives;
Audacious and Adamant: The Story of Maverick Alberta, accompanies
it. Van Herk's words accompany George Webber's photographs in *In
This Place: Calgary 2004–2011* and *Prairie Gothic*.

RUSSELL WANGERSKY is a writer, editor, and columnist from
St. John's, Newfoundland and Labrador. His books include the
firefighting memoir *Burning Down the House: Fighting Fires and Losing
Myself* (2008), the novel *The Glass Harmonica* (2010), and the short-
story collections *The Hour of Bad Decisions* (2006), and *Whirl Away*
(2012), which was shortlisted for the Scotiabank Giller Prize.

CASSY WELBURN is a poet and storyteller who has had her work
published in *FreeFall Magazine*, *The Antigonish Review*, and a variety
of anthologies, as well as broadcast on CBC radio. She enjoys sharing
her work at storycafés and festivals around Canada.

MADELAINE WONG is a former schoolteacher who now dedicates
her time to writing and caring for her family. She has been published
in the *Copperfield Review*, *Dark Gothic Resurrected*, and *Toska Magazine*
and won *FreeFall Magazine*'s chapbook contest in 2010. She self-
published her mother's biography, *Cradling the Past: A Biography of
Margaret Shaw*. When she was a shy teenager, Wong's imagination
was fired by the adventure, violence, and magic of Roman and Greek
mythology, and the ancient myths continue to influence her writing.

ELAINE WOO facilitates writing classes for *Megaphone Magazine*'s
Community Program. She is membership coordinator for CWILA

(Canadian Women in the Literary Arts). She recently published in *Arc*, *poetrypacific.blogspot.com*, *Ricepaper*, *V6A*, *Earthwalk*, and *The Enpipe Line*, and was shortlisted for the 2012 City of Vancouver Book Award. Her art-song collaboration, "Night-time Symphony," with composer Daniel Marshall earned a festival prize from the Boston Metro Opera in early 2013.

ELIZABETH ZOTOVA Only child, Siberian-born introvert. Domestically inclined. Likes Scrabble, wine, fruit trees, and spoiling her parrots with reckless abandon.

Permissions

Alex Boyd's "The Culture of Shyness" was previously published in *The Least Important Man* (Biblioasis, 2012). Reprinted by permission of the publisher.

Janis Butler Holm's "Are You an Introvert? Take This Simple Quiz" was previously published in *Sketch* (No. 1, 2009).

Weyman Chan's "that animal" and "to the red-haired girl on eighth" were previously published in *Chinese Blue* (Talonbooks, 2012). Reprinted by permission of the publisher.

Lorna Crozier's "Watching My Lover" was previously published in *The Blue Hour of the Day* (McClelland & Stewart, 2007). Reprinted by permission of the publisher.

Steven Heighton's "Drunk Judgement" was previously published in *Poetry* (Vol. 189, No. 5, 2007) and *The Address Book* (Anansi, 2004). Reprinted by permission of the publisher.

Steven Heighton's "Silentium" was previously published in *Arc* (No. 60, Summer 2008) and *Patient Frame* (Anansi, 2010). Reprinted by permission of the publisher.

Shawna Lemay's "Shybrightly" was previously published under the title "Shy" in *Prairie Fire* (Vol. 26, No. 3, Autumn 2005).

Naomi K. Lewis's "Say Water" was previously published in *Prairie Fire* (Vol. 31, No. 2, Summer 2010).

Micheline Maylor's "Insecurity" was previously published in *Whirr & Click* (Frontenac House, 2013). Reprinted by permission of the publisher.

Don McKay's "Sometimes a Voice (2)" was previously published in *Field Marks: The Poetry of Don McKay*, ed. Méira Cook (Wilfrid Laurier University Press, 2006). Reprinted by permission of the publisher.

Natalie Simpson's "affect Thrum" was previously published in *filling Station* (No. 51, 2012).